POETS IN BRIEF

THOMAS LOVELL BEDDOES

T0382068

THOMAS LOVELL BEDDOES
An Anthology

Chosen by

F. L. LUCAS
Fellow of King's College
Cambridge

CAMBRIDGE
AT THE UNIVERSITY PRESS
1932

CAMBRIDGE
UNIVERSITY PRESS

University Printing House, Cambridge CB2 8BS, United Kingdom

Published in the United States of America by Cambridge University Press, New York

Cambridge University Press is part of the University of Cambridge.

It furthers the University's mission by disseminating knowledge in the pursuit of
education, learning and research at the highest international levels of excellence.

www.cambridge.org
Information on this title: www.cambridge.org/9781107652446

© Cambridge University Press 1932

First published 1932
First paperback edition 2014

A catalogue record for this publication is available from the British Library

ISBN 978-1-107-65244-6 Paperback

To

GEORGE BARNES

PREFACE

It is my hope that this selection may introduce to a wider circle of readers a poet still too little known. With few writers is there a stronger case for an anthology. His letters are not easily accessible; his best poetry lies scattered through those chaotic plays which he found it so easy to begin, so hard to finish. Even when he did finish them, their value lies not in their dramatic qualities as wholes, but in their splendid moments; and many of his loveliest things appear as "Fragments" even in the collected edition. Yet at his best he can write with an intensity of imagination unsurpassed since Shakespeare.

I have included a little of his juvenile play, *The Brides' Tragedy*; a full selection from *Death's Jest-Book*, his main work, which contains, however, a good deal of "sad stuff"; most of the unfinished *Second Brother*; and every word that remains of the magnificent *Torrismond*, which Beddoes never carried beyond the first line of Act II. The rest of the book consists of a selection from the highly characteristic letters, other dramatic fragments, and a few lyrics.

I have to thank *Life and Letters* for permission to reprint as Introduction here an article on Beddoes published in October, 1930; and Dr Philip Gosse, Messrs J. M. Dent & Sons, Ltd., and Messrs Elkin Mathews & Marrot for permission to reprint copyright material.

F. L. L.

KING'S COLLEGE
CAMBRIDGE

December 1931

CONTENTS

INTRODUCTION

"Alors s'assit sur un monde en ruines une jeunesse soucieuse.... Et ils parlèrent tant et si longtemps, que toutes les illusions humaines, comme des arbres en automne, tombaient feuille à feuille autour d'eux, et que ceux qui les écoutaient passaient leur main sur leur front, comme des fiévreux qui s'éveillent." This is not a picture of post-war Europe; at least, not of our post-war Europe. The words are all but a century old. Thus wrote de Musset, middle-aged already in his twenties, just as Byron had been "a perfect Timon, not nineteen". Even in his impudent little comedies, at moments, the same cry of anguish makes itself suddenly heard. "Ce que tu dis là," exclaims Fantasio's friend, "ferait rire bien des gens; moi, cela me fait frémir; c'est l'histoire du siècle entier. L'éternité est une grande aire, d'où tous les siècles, comme de jeunes aiglons, se sont envolés tour à tour pour traverser le ciel et disparaître; le nôtre est arrivé à son tour au bord du nid; mais on lui a coupé les ailes, et il attend la mort en regardant l'espace dans lequel il ne peut s'élancer."

It was no mere affectation. No doubt youth is often affected; but youth is also often bitterly sincere. No doubt it was a mood; it passed, as moods do; but it is curious to find that the last century, which we tend to picture as populated by brisk business men with a blind confidence in God, themselves, and Progress, could be in its early twenties, as well as in its nineties, thus *fin-de-siècle*. Yet can we wonder? There are dawns, indeed, when to be young is "very heaven"; the morning after is apt to be less celestial. Then the young pass from excessive enthusiasm to excessive melancholy, feeling that they have been born out of due time and are making their first bow on a stage where all is over.

It was natural that the generation which came to birth with the nineteenth century should feel this disillusion. There seemed nothing but a puppet-show left in progress in the theatre of the world. It had been otherwise for their fathers. The Werthers had forgotten their own sorrows as they beheld the earth alight with Liberty, and the Rights of Man coming in glory on the clouds of Heaven. Like clouds, indeed, those Rights had vanished; in their place had risen in the same year, 1804, the pale stars of *René* and *Obermann*; but in their place also had ensued for twenty years, terrible and yet magnificently Titanic, a Battle of the Gods. Full disillusion was kept at bay. War was still romantic then, however misguidedly; a field for genius, not merely for the muddling mediocrities that floundered through the slime of our last conflict. Some may recall the vivid narrative of a Piedmontese private in the Grande Armée—how, at the mere sight of that short grey-coated figure riding down the line before Moscow, he found himself breathing as hard as if he had been running, and bathed in sweat amid the cold of a Russian winter's day. It was not thus that we felt about the Generals of 1916. But after the romance, and then the epic, there followed now this poor farce of rejuvenated kings and reactionary governments. This

was what the generation that had heard through boy-
hood the guns of Austerlitz and Jena and Wagram, sat
down to contemplate, as they and the century together
came of age. And so there were other caged eaglets
in these years besides the Duc de Reichstadt; other
smouldering firebrands, lit too late, besides the heroes
of Stendhal. The enormous energy of a Balzac, a
Dumas, a Hugo might go trampling onward under
that leaden sky, after the last baleful splendour of
Byron had fallen from it like a final meteor; but others
of the young, with less vitality, felt weighed down by
this load of emotional, as well as political, reaction.
Smaller writers, like Maxime du Camp, bear out de
Musset's description; and though in England, so much
less touched by the war and now at length victorious,
we should not expect the same aftermath, it may be
more than coincidence that so few writers are to-day
remembered who were not either over twenty-five or
under twelve—too old or too young to be vitally im-
pressionable—when the year 1820 closed. In prose,
between Carlyle (born in 1795) and Thackeray (born
in 1811) the only names of any note are Macaulay (who
would have been hard to damp in any age), Mill,
Newman, and George Borrow. Similarly there is a gap
in the lineage of English poets between the birth of
Keats in 1795 and that of Tennyson in 1809. Such
speculation about literary vintage-years must remain
fanciful; yet there is one poet born between Keats and
Tennyson who was certainly cramped by a despondency
like de Musset's, due in part, no doubt, to his own
temperament, but partly also, I believe, to his time.

been his fag. Two of these details have been repeated by
Sir Edmund Gosse and Mr Lytton Strachey—the boy's
habit of declaiming speeches from Elizabethan drama
at the little Bevan (who was forcibly enlisted as accom-
plice, enemy, or mistress) with a rain of kicks or caresses
as required; and his vengeance on a certain locksmith,
whose bad work was repaid with a dramatic interlude
composed and recited for his benefit, and depicting his
death-bed of horror-stricken remorse, his funeral, and
his consignment by a legion of devils to the Bottomless
Pit. But there are other less-known anecdotes from
the same source, too characteristic, I think, to be for-
gotten. The inborn oddity, the rebelliousness, the eld-
ritch humour, the Gothic grotesqueness, the love of
Elizabethan poetry, the strange mastery of words—all
these qualities of the poet we know, are already
shadowed here at Charterhouse. Already he dominated
his fellows; the nicknames he invented stuck like burs;
his defiance, too, of authority had already begun. When
the traditional liberty to play hockey in the cloisters
was abolished, young Beddoes, who normally never
played at all, appeared to lead one side in the now for-
bidden game, his head bedizened with feathers and his
body adorned by a paste-board shield where shone
emblazoned a clenched fist, with the motto: "Manus
haec inimica tyrannis". This demonstration proved
too much for the gravity of the authorities and the
prohibition was dissolved in laughter. But if Beddoes
could uphold the oppressed, he could also do his share
of oppression. Readers of *The Newcomes* will recall
how the old pensioners at Charterhouse were called

he had written poems on Alexander's Invasion of India
in the manner of *The Loves of the Plants*, novels on
the reform of drunken labourers, political pamphlets,
designs for Rational Toys, *Considerations on the Medi-
cinal Use and on the Production of Factitious Airs*,
A Guide for Self-Preservation and Parental Affection,
Good Advice for the Husbandman in Harvest, papers on
basalt, on the abuses of the Bodleian Library, on the
curl in potatoes. Like Browning, he had been one that
"marched breast forward". True, it is not easy to
march in any other way—a point which Browning
seems not to have quite considered; but at all events
Dr Beddoes marched; and discovered on the road
many odd, and some useful, things.[1] But when we
turn to his son, the author of *Death's Jest-Book*, the
contrast is complete. In every apple of his Tree of
Knowledge lay a little black wriggling worm of doubt.
More gifted as an anatomist, said Blumenbach, than
any pupil he had had for fifty years—as dazzling a
poet, in his sudden flashes, as the whole century
brought forth—he yet perished by his own hand at
forty-five, leaving to Dr Ecklin a stomach-pump and
to the world only a wild heap of poetic fragments,
blood and sawdust mixed with diamonds.

Left fatherless in his sixth year, the boy was sent at
fourteen to Charterhouse. Long afterwards, when Bed-
does was dead, his friend Kelsall extracted strange tales
of his doings there from a certain C. D. Bevan who had

[1] For a fuller account of this eccentric and indefatigable
figure I may refer the reader to an article in *Life and Letters*
for January, 1930.

been his fag. Two of these details have been repeated by Sir Edmund Gosse and Mr Lytton Strachey—the boy's habit of declaiming speeches from Elizabethan drama at the little Bevan (who was forcibly enlisted as accomplice, enemy, or mistress) with a rain of kicks or caresses as required; and his vengeance on a certain locksmith, whose bad work was repaid with a dramatic interlude composed and recited for his benefit, and depicting his death-bed of horror-stricken remorse, his funeral, and his consignment by a legion of devils to the Bottomless Pit. But there are other less-known anecdotes from the same source, too characteristic, I think, to be forgotten. The inborn oddity, the rebelliousness, the eldritch humour, the Gothic grotesqueness, the love of Elizabethan poetry, the strange mastery of words—all these qualities of the poet we know, are already shadowed here at Charterhouse. Already he dominated his fellows; the nicknames he invented stuck like burs; his defiance, too, of authority had already begun. When the traditional liberty to play hockey in the cloisters was abolished, young Beddoes, who normally never played at all, appeared to lead one side in the now forbidden game, his head bedizened with feathers and his body adorned by a paste-board shield where shone emblazoned a clenched fist, with the motto: "Manus haec inimica tyrannis". This demonstration proved too much for the gravity of the authorities and the prohibition was dissolved in laughter. But if Beddoes could uphold the oppressed, he could also do his share of oppression. Readers of *The Newcomes* will recall how the old pensioners at Charterhouse were called

"Codds", and Colonel Newcome himself, "Codd
Colonel". Three of these old brethren the young Bed-
does particularly loved to torment—"Codd Curio",
whom he called so because he collected curiosities;
"Codd Frolicsome", a Trafalgar veteran who had
St Vitus's dance; and "Codd Sine-breech" who was
slightly crazed in the head. These old gentlemen, who
were attended by the most Gampish of nurses, suffered
such persecutions from their enemy that Codd Sine-
breech was fain to hire a drummer of the Guards as
reinforcement. Hostilities were not, however, con-
tinuous; every now and then both sides indulged in
armistice feasts of oysters and lobsters, gin and porter,
at which Beddoes would dance or give some of his
dramatic recitations. Another prank of his was to pur-
loin all the fire-irons from the kitchen of the preacher's
house, so that the infuriated cook went about cursing
in a vain search for his pokers, tongs, and shovels;
these were mysteriously restored at midnight, tied
round the neck of Beddoes's fag, who was himself tied
to the door-knocker with a resulting din, as the little
boy struggled there, like a dozen coal-scuttles falling
downstairs.

The same familiar imp of insubordination attended
Beddoes to Pembroke College, Oxford, where he
treated his fellows with cold aloofness and the college
authorities, by Bevan's account, with "a course of
studied impertinence". On one occasion, we are told,
a lecturer, tired of seeing him sitting and glowering in
complete inattention, exclaimed: "I wish you would
at least cut your book, Mr Beddoes"; at once the

young man rose, walked out, and returned with the largest butcher's cleaver money could buy, with which he proceeded to do as requested. The ensuing uproar brought the lecture to an untimely end. Few, too, who have come upon it, will forget that deadly stab, that poisoned "jewel five words long", in one of his Oxford letters: "Mr Milman (our poetry professor) has made me quite unfashionable here by denouncing me as 'one of a villainous school'. *I wish him another son*".

Such things are slight, no doubt. But only in such glimpses does Beddoes loom upon us for moments, like a lurid fog-bound sun, out of the mists which have engulfed for ever the secrets of his inner life. We catch sight of the young poet, with his strange physical resemblance to Keats, helping to print the posthumous verse of the still neglected Shelley, whose aery spirit had so strange an appeal for his own earthy one; or scribbling imitations of Elizabethan drama with a power that seems to spring from him full-grown; or stealthily hacking the pages of his first published volume from the bindings of the copies on his friends' shelves. Then there appears for a moment the young law-student, working at Southampton under that most poetic of solicitors, Kelsall, who was to struggle with heroic resistance to keep alive the memory of Beddoes's work for a generation after its author's death and up to the eve of his own; next, the young doctor, learning to prefer "Apollo's pillbox to his lyre" and Germany to England; growing into a stoic, prosaic, grim anatomist, and yet still turning at instants from skull and scalpel to retouch the everlasting *Death's*

Jest-Book; and last of all the obscure revolutionary, hunted from Bavaria to Zürich, from Zürich back to Germany, then deported in turn from Hanover, from Prussia, and from Bavaria once more. He has by now almost forgotten his country; his rare visits only inflame his indifference into active irritation with "this dull, idle, pampered isle". He has become more and more bizarre; his talk shows a morbid preoccupation with death's-heads and skeletons; sisters and cousins object to his habits of lying in bed all day, drinking perhaps (or, as he called it, "having neuralgia"), and then prowling like a spectre about the house all night. He arrived at the residence of one relative at Cheney Longville in Shropshire mounted, it is said, upon an ass. Was he sane, this sombre recluse whom the Procters one evening found struggling with the attendants at Drury Lane Theatre, which he had been trying to set on fire by holding a lighted five-pound note under a chair? There must have been sighs of relief among the Beddoeses of Bristol and Birkenhead when this disreputable relative went back to cutting up dead Germans at Frankfurt. There he now lost his health, by pricking his hand during a dissection; and lost his heart in addition to a young baker called Degen, whom he was set on turning into an actor, hiring the theatre at Zürich for him to play Hotspur. The rest is well known. The inhabitants of Zürich looked coldly on the heroics of Herr Degen; Degen in his turn grew cold towards Beddoes and went back to his dough in Frankfurt. The poet, bearded now and looking "like Shakespeare", removed in deep despondency to Basel, where he tried to kill himself, first by stabbing his leg, then by tearing off the bandages in hospital, until the limb gangrened and had to be amputated. He recovered, in body, and seemingly in mind as well; Degen, too, had been persuaded to return to him. Yet as soon as he was well enough to go out, he took the opportunity to procure poison, came back to the hospital, and died unconscious the same night (26th January 1849). In his bosom lay a pencilled bequest of a stomach-pump and a case of champagne: "I am food for what I am good for— worms...I ought to have been among other things a good poet. Life was too great a bore on one peg and that a bad one".

But though Death's Jester lay now quiet at last in the cypress-shade of the hospital-cemetery at Zürich, the jest was not ended. His works remained, to become in their turn the tennis-balls of chance. His family wanted them safely destroyed—all except those of a harmless medical nature. Only Zoe King, the cousin who is said to have felt for him an attachment he could not return, and the faithful Kelsall resisted this proposal; and, through Kelsall, *Death's Jest-Book* appeared in 1850, followed a year later by a volume of poems. But a new generation of writers had appeared by now; and the world of 1850, watching the birth in swift succession of works like *David Copperfield*, *Wuthering Heights*, and *In Memoriam*, had no eyes for this odd relic of the unknown dead. Only a few observers saw that something new had been added to English poetry; but among them were Tennyson and Browning. Years passed; Kelsall, devoted as ever, heard of Browning's admiration, met him (1867), begged him to write a preface for a new edition, sent him some of the manuscripts, offered to bequeath him all. Browning accepted; he contemplated, at a time when he seemed likely to be made Professor of Poetry at Oxford, giving his opening lecture on Beddoes. But nothing came of it, neither preface nor lecture; Browning had grown bored; and Kelsall, too, was growing old. In 1869 he made, with Zoe King, a pilgrimage to the scenes at Basel and Zürich where Beddoes's life had guttered out twenty years before; in July 1872 he contributed an article on the dead poet to the *Fortnightly*; three months after this "last stroke for Beddoes", as he called it, he too was dead.

The manuscripts duly passed to Browning, with a message from Mrs Kelsall revealing to him what had been hitherto kept dark—that Beddoes had died by his own hand. This grim addition made the poet of optimism more disposed than ever to play ostrich and forget the whole affair. The box of yellowing papers acquired in his eyes a sinister horror. Another decade went by; then he talked of it to his young neighbour, Edmund Gosse; and finally, one day in 1883, led him to the locked box, pressed the key into his hand, and fled. However, once Bluebeard's Cupboard was open, Browning's repugnance weakened sufficiently for him to read over the manuscripts with Gosse; who in consequence produced a new edition of the *Works* in 1890, followed by a volume of the poet's *Letters* in 1894. But, half a century after his death, misfortune still dogged Beddoes. The edition was perfunctorily carried out; and the manuscripts, returned to Browning's son in Italy, disappeared in the confusion that followed his death. What became of them remains to this day obscure; there seems no basis for the story once told, that "Pen" Browning's servants ransacked their dead master's house, and that no one knew what scented tresses of some dark Italian beauty, faded now in their turn, the papers of Beddoes might have perished at last to curl. Finally, three years ago (1928), Gosse produced a grandiose new edition of the Letters and Poetical Works, ornamented with decorations from Holbein's Dance of Death; but before its completion he too died; and with this new edition reappeared, alas, the errors and corruptions and mutilations of the old. Beddoes might well have laughed in his grave.

Not that it is much easier to know what the poet was really like, than what he really did. The letters are eccentric, cold, impersonal—all the more impersonal for being filled with a great deal of bitter badinage. His jests serve him, one feels, for shield as well as sword. That sardonic smile makes his face more than ever of a mask. Poetry, Anatomy, Liberty—he pursued each in turn, to disillusion at the last. There is little trace in his life of affection, apart from the mysterious Degen: "I fear I am a non-conductor of friendship, a not-very-likeable person, so that I must make sure of my own respect". And yet this coldness has an air of being studied rather than natural. There is a Byronic pose in his saturnine description of his behaviour on a voyage to Hamburg—how he "re-

mained impenetrably proud and silent every wave of
the way, dropping now and then a little venom into
the mixture of conversation to make it effervesce";
and this impassivity is belied by passages in his poetry
of a quivering tenderness:

> Your love was much,
> Your life but an inhabitant of his.

> Cyrano, Cyrano,
> I yearn, and thirst, and ache to be beloved,
> As I could love,—through my eternal soul,
> Immutably, immortally, intensely,
> Immeasurably. Oh! I am not at home
> In this December world, with men of ice,
> Cold sirs and madams. That I had a heart,
> By whose warm throbs of love to set my soul!
> I tell thee I have not begun to live,
> I'm not myself, till I've another self
> To lock my dearest, and most secret thoughts in;
> Change petty faults, and whispering pardons with;
> Sweetly to rule, and Oh! most sweetly serve.

Surely, if the writer of that lived withdrawn into his
shell, it was precisely because he was sensitive, and had
suffered. He seems as if part of him had perished
young: his very portrait as an undergraduate has a
mummy-like air; he resembles his own Wolfram, a
dead thing in a living world, gentle once but hardened
now. Certainly the letters show him, if no lover, at
all events a good hater. He has a particular dislike
of British Philistinism, whether in individuals like
"Mr Milman", or in the nation as a whole:

Drink, Britannia! Britannia, drink your tea,
For Britons, bores, and buttered toast, they all begins with B.

O flattering likeness on a copper coin,
Sit still upon your slave-raised cotton ball
With upright toasting-fork and toothless cat.

But, for that matter, the whole world sickens him: "I am now so thoroughly penetrated with the conviction of the absurdity and unsatisfactory nature of human life, that I search with avidity for every shadow of a proof or probability of an after-existence both in the material and immaterial nature of man". One may wonder that a mind which found this life so tedious, should so sigh for eternity; but in such matters the human temperament is seldom very logical. Gnawed by the worm on earth, it speculates hopefully about the worm that never dies.

Still, if the letters throw but a glimmer on the poet's heart, they reveal very clearly those two qualities of his brain which go to make his poetry at times so astonishing—imagination and wit. Even as a child, his first favourite poet had been Cowley. And to read these letters brings home with fresh force how hardy a plant real originality is. Such a mind, read what it may, imitate whom it will, imposes as invincibly as a distorting mirror its own queer quality on all its reflections. It was a gift Sterne had; it belongs in our own day to Mr E. M. Forster—who else but he would behold the United States, for example, with the most spontaneously innocent air in the world, as a brightly-coloured apron tied chastely round the buxom waist of the American Continent? So with Beddoes. He too was born with this gift of seeing in every square a fifth corner; no doubt he cultivated his oddity, finding it succeed; but it always seems a natural part of him, as if he had had a mandrake for a comforter in the cradle and made it his youthful hobby "to chat with mummies in a pyramid, and breakfast on basilisk's eggs". "There is nothing of interest in town", he will write, "except a pair of live crocodiles in St Martin's Lane." "I will sacrifice my raven to you", he answers, when Kelsall recoils from the sinister menagerie of *Death's Jest-Book*, "but my crocky is really very dear to me." This is, indeed, one of the few expressions of affection in his whole correspondence. Or again: "Such verses as these and their brethren, will never be preserved to be pasted on the inside of the coffin of our planet". Such excessive preoccupation with the macabre may seem affected; yet the reader who looks back at that cadaverous portrait, and forward to the last scene at Zürich, must surely admit that the affectation, if such it was, went deep. But his fancy does not always glimmer thus coldly like a glow-worm on a grave: its flames can dance gaily enough, if still perhaps with a slight breath of sulphur: "Dear Kelsall. I have been in the native land of the unicorn about a week....I had no time to visit Procter...but am told that he is appointed to a high office in the government of the kingdom of ye moon"; such is Beddoes's way of conveying his own arrival in England and Procter's new Commissionership of Lunacy. Or he will write home of a castle at Göttingen: "The date of the tower is said to be 963: if this be true, it may have earned a citizenship among the semi-eternal stony populace of the planet; at all events it will be older than some hills

which pretend to be natural and carry trees and houses".
Just so might another metaphysical physician have
brooded two centuries before; we should feel how
typical was the thought in a letter written home by Sir
Thomas Browne to Norwich. But there is a more
flashing fancy than Browne's at work in Beddoes's
vivid description of fireflies at Milan: "as if the swift
wheeling of the earth struck fire out of the black
atmosphere; as if the winds were being set upon this
planetary grindstone, and gave out such momentary
sparks from their edges". It might be a description
of his own poetry. How many poets one might search
from cover to cover without finding anything as
brilliant as this round grindstone of a world!

Those, then, who know the poetry of Beddoes will
have no difficulty in recognizing the fainter shadow
of his genius that lies across the pages of the letters;
but there is one more disillusion here than even the
poems show—disillusion about his poetry itself. He
early expresses a sense of failure; he feels that he is
trying to animate a corpse, that he is but the ghost of
an Elizabethan dramatist, squeaking and gibbering
plays fit only for audiences long lapped in their winding-
sheets. "The man who is to awaken the drama", he
writes of a *remaniement* of Massinger's *Fatal Dowry*,
"must be a bold trampling fellow—no creeper in
worm-holes—no reviser even, however good. These
reanimations are vampire-cold—we want to see some-
thing that our great-grandsires did not know." He
must have felt the relevance of that judgment to him-
self; and if he is severe on his contemporaries, pro-

phesying after Shelley's death "nothing but fog, rain, blight in due succession", he is still harder on his own work: "I am essentially unpoetical in character, habits, and ways of thinking: and nothing but the desperate hunger for distinction so common to young gentlemen at the University ever set me upon rhyming" (rather in the same way, it may be remembered, he denied himself a heart). *Death's Jest-Book* he dismisses as "unentertaining, unamiable, and utterly unpopular". He finds himself wanting in the two indispensable qualities of a dramatist, "power of drawing character, and humour"; indeed at moments he feels "doubt of my aptitude for any higher literary or commercial occupation"; he cannot even finish his plays—"as usual I have begun a new tragedy"; "a new tragic abortion of mine has absolutely extended its fœtus to a quarter of the fourth act"; "those three acts, which I cannot possibly show to any eye but that of Vulcan, are absolutely worthless". What wonder if this hesitating Prince of Denmark begot no second *Hamlet*, but only dramatic fragments and brilliant incoherences?

And yet I know no poet whose poetic moments are more crammed with poetry. How much one values this sort of spasmodic writer depends on temperament —whether one is "classical" and asks for ordered beauty of form, or "romantic" and cares for flashes of dazzling colour. But, after all, why not love both? Beddoes can only give the second kind of pleasure; but he gives it so intensely, that I feel he is undervalued still. What he needs is a good selection of short passages, often of single lines. The anthologists have merely concentrated on a few of his lyrics, which have the sort of prettiness dear to their pussy-cat mentalities; just as they persist in representing, or misrepresenting, the author of *The City of Dreadful Night* by the cockney amenities of "Sunday up the River". As a lyric poet Beddoes can be lovely; but it is in his verse dialogue that he shows his strength—not only that power of phrase and image with which his letters vibrate, but something also that they could not reveal —his mastery, even rarer, perhaps, of that Proteus among metrical forms, so simple-seeming, so mockingly elusive in a hundred poets' hands—dramatic blank verse.

The strange thing is that his most living poetry is a pastiche of dead work. As a contemporary of Keats, writing in the manner of 1820, he is usually unreadable; it is as a contemporary of Webster, risen from the dust of two centuries, that he quickens into a quivering vitality. His Muse is a Witch of Endor, her magic a necromantic gift of waking to utterance a tongue long buried. Yet this becomes a little less strange when we remember how Chatterton too, hopeless when he writes in the poetic style of 1770, found himself only by escaping back to an England older still than Beddoes ever revisited. And think, too, of the whole Renaissance with its aping of the classics. There are poets who can write vitally of, and in the style of, their own age; there remain others for whom it is equally essential to escape from it. Generations of critics have lost their heads and tempers squabbling which is right. Surely both are. Surely it is understandable that a poet may wish to break away to some magic islet of his own, where he can feel himself monarch of all he surveys, because he shares it only with the dead. For they do not cramp our style as the living can; we can learn from them without fearing to become too imitatively like them; and the older the dead, the easier they are to elbow aside when we turn to write ourselves, as if their ghosts wore thinner and more shadowy with the years. Distance can lend enchantment also to the voice.

At all events it is on borrowed plumes that Beddoes soars his highest, and when masquerading as a Jacobean that he seems most himself. No one else since Dryden has so recaptured the splendour of blank verse as a medium for dialogue, escaping that marmoreal stiffness which Milton brought. For it is, indeed, almost as if the author of *Paradise Lost* had turned the verse of *Hamlet* into stone; to be carved and built by him and others after him into shapes of monumental nobility, but never again to seem like living flesh and blood, as once in Elizabethan hands. Milton's "organ-voice" has no *vox humana*; and musical as a Wordsworth or a Tennyson may be, Shakespeare's Cleopatra speaks what has since become, rhythmically, a dead language.

Beddoes alone seems to me to have rediscovered the full secret of varied stress and fingering, feminine ending and resolved foot in all their elasticity. His lines run rippling like wind along the corn: his Muse moves like his own Valeria—

> She goes with her light feet, still as the sparrow
> Over the air, or through the grass its shade.

All the stranger is the contrast which combines with this perfect grace of rhythm such a grimness of ideas; until his verse recalls that tragic conception of the Greek—the Gorgon Medusa, "the beautiful horror", the lovely lips twisted with eternal pain:

> I have seen the mottled tigress
> Sport with her cubs as tenderly and gay
> As Lady Venus with her kitten Cupids.

So, too, the Muse of Beddoes, dagger and poison-cup in hand, goes gliding on her way with the light feet and swaying grace of Herrick's loves in their wild civility:

> The snake that loves the twilight is come out,
> Beautiful, still, and deadly.

> But now some lamp awakes,
> And with the venom of a basilisk's wink
> Burns the dark winds.

> O that the twenty coming years were over!
> Then should I be at rest, where ruined arches
> Shut out the troublesome, unghostly day,
> And idlers might be sitting on my tomb,
> Telling how I did die.

> You're young and must be merry in the world,
> Have friends to envy, lovers to betray you,
> And feed young children with the blood of your heart,
> Till they have sucked up strength enough to break it.

> I will go search about for Comfort,
> Him that enrobed in mouldering cerements sits
> At the grey tombstone's head, beneath the yew;
> Men call him Death, but Comfort is his name.

The poison is given with a caress: the dagger tickles before it plunges home. It is interesting to compare the

rhythm of Beddoes with the dramatic verse of another
master of the metre in its statelier narrative form,
Tennyson:

> I once was out with Henry in the days
> When Henry loved me, and we came upon
> A wild-fowl sitting on her nest, so still
> I reach'd my hand and touched; she did not stir;
> The snow had frozen round her, and she sat
> Stone-dead upon a heap of ice-cold eggs.
> Look how this love, this mother, runs through all
> The world God made—even the beast—the bird!

Any ear must notice the difference. Not only are the
individual lines in Tennyson more regular and so more
monotonous, and also slower through their avoidance
of the feminine endings or extra syllables which lend
speed to a verse like:

> And feed young children with the blood of your heart;

they also for the same reason refuse to coalesce with
one another into a verse-paragraph, in spite of the
author's effort to make them do so by ending his lines
with words like "upon". Each decasyllable somehow
persists in scanning itself separately with a sort of
conscious pride in its own virtuous avoidance of any
undue licence. It is as if the passage were being written
by a poetical type-writer, which very beautifully rang
a little silver bell at the close of each line, and pulled
itself elaborately back to begin each new one; whereas
Beddoes has the sinuous onward gliding of a living
adder through the grass. Open Webster:

> O Men
> That lye upon your death-beds, and are haunted
> With howling wives, neere trust them, they'le re-marry

> Ere the worme pierce your winding sheete: ere the Spider
> Make a thinne curtaine for your Epitaphes.

The kinship needs no pointing out; metrically, indeed, Beddoes may often seem even nearer to the slightly decadent softness of Fletcher or Shirley than to Webster's harsher rhythm; but in his diction he shows the same swift and bitter strength:

> I have huddled her into the wormy earth.

> Let Heaven unscabbard each star-hilted lightning.

> If you would wound your foe,
> Get swords that pierce the mind; a bodily slice
> Is cured with *surgeon's butter*.

Of the two supreme excellences of Beddoes, then, as a poet, this power of rhythm and of phrase seems to me one; the other is his sheer force of imagination. He has ideas that are poetic in and by themselves quite apart from their expression; like the silence of Ajax before Odysseus in Hades, like the symbols of Ibsen in his later plays. Indeed, the cry Beddoes wrings from the lips of one of his characters might well be his own:

> I'll go brood
> And strain my burning and distracted soul
> Against the naked spirit of the world
> Till some portent's begotten.

It is a typically "metaphysical" conception. Yet he escapes that frigid ingenuity which has so often been fatal to poets of this kind, in the seventeenth century, and in the twentieth—clever persons, who have yet been so simple as to suppose that their creations could live and breathe without a heart. Thus Beddoes, thinking of Noah's Deluge, sees it, characteristically enough, through the eye of the daisy on which its first raindrop fell; but he feels also for the daisy itself with the tenderness of Burns.

> I should not say
> How thou art like the daisy in Noah's meadow
> On which the foremost drop of rain fell warm
> And soft at evening; so the little flower
> Wrapped up its leaves, and shut the treacherous water
> Close to the golden welcome of its breast.

Time itself may be twisted by his visionary hands into a thing of space, with all the tortured ingenuity of a Donne—and yet one does not really have a sense of torture, so much does his mind seem at home in its own strange labyrinths:

> I have said that Time
> Is a great river running to Eternity.
> Methinks 'tis all one water, and the fragments
> That crumble off our ever-dwindling life,
> Dropping into it, first make the twelve-houred circle,
> And that spreads outward to the great round Ever.

Or again:

> I begin to hear
> Strange but sweet sounds, and the loud rocky dashing
> Of waves where Time into Eternity
> Falls over ruined worlds.

It is this unusual power of at once thinking so abstractly and seeing so concretely, that makes him a master of the macabre. For the macabre only too easily becomes a little vulgar: Poe can be frightful in quite another sense of the word than he intended.

Cemeteries are no very healthy dancing-ground for the Muses, and not much real music has been got from bones. But Beddoes, though he has his lapses, has learnt that the hinted can be far more terrible than the crudely said. In one of his scenes, for instance, a festive gathering is haunted by spectres:

> There were more shadows there, than there were men.

Or again, a plague-infected air becomes, before his vision,

> Transparent as the glass of poisoned water
> Through which the drinker sees his murderer smiling.

What a concentrated brevity of horror is there—as if the picture were drawn on the thumbnail of the assassin! Or again, the earth's roundness—what is its cause? The answer of Beddoes is all his own:

> Ay, to this end the earth is made a ball—
> Else, crawling to the brink, despair would plunge
> Into the infinite eternal air
> And leave its sorrows and its sins behind.

Here is the old melancholy of Burton, with his speculations on the space Hell occupies in the globe's interior, fermenting in a more modern mind. Why, again, have ghosts and apparitions ceased? There is the same fantastic ingenuity in Beddoes's reply, and the same wild eloquence:

> To trust in story,
> In the old times Death was a feverish sleep,
> In which men walked. The other world was cold
> And thinly peopled, so life's emigrants
> Came back to mingle with the crowds of earth.

> But, now great cities are transplanted thither,
> Memphis and Babylon and either Thebes
> And Priam's towery town with its one beech,
> The dead are most and merriest: so be sure
> There'll be no more haunting till their towns
> Are full to the garret: then they'll shut their gates
> To keep the living out.

Such concreteness of vision combined with passionate concentration of speech—it is these two qualities in Beddoes that lend the hiss of an arrow to his single lines of scorn:

> The shallow, tasteless skimmings of their love...
>
> And scratched it on your leaden memories...
>
> And lay thee, worm, where thou shalt multiply.

Indeed, nothing in him has so much the air of being written *con amore*, as these hot gusts from a furnace-mouth of hatred; it is as if he had taken to himself that cry of one of his characters:

> Unmilk me of my mother, and pour in
> Salt scorn and steaming hate.

The passions he deals in may be often poisoned, but they are at least passion; and lack of that might easily have become the besetting weakness of a poet with so much sheer cleverness, as it is to-day with the young who set out to imitate Donne's ingenuity without his intensity, in a way that suggests Blake's Lamb trying to frisk itself into the likeness of Blake's Tiger. Cleverness, it seems to me, has its place in poetry, but only a second place, as the tiring-maid of passion or of beauty; and the cleverness of Beddoes makes his loveliness not inferior, but a more complex, artificial thing than that of Wordsworth's Lucy or Tennyson's Mariana. Not for him

> The silence that is in the starry sky,
> The sleep that is among the lonely hills,

but

> Crescented night and amethystine stars.

A violet is not for him a simple violet; it is like

> Pandora's eye
> When first it darkened with immortal life;

(as if life, like death—or even more than death, per-haps—threw a sad shadow when it came). A pine-tree across the moon turns into a river before his agile gaze:

> One snowy cloud
> Hangs like an avalanche of frozen light
> Upon the peak of night's cerulean Alp,
> And yon still pine, a bleak anatomy,
> Flows like a river on the planet's disk
> With its black wandering arms.

(And there are persons who deny a visual imagination to be needed for enjoying poetry!) Even a moonlit water-drop holds for him within it the semblance of a world's unhappiness:

> For what is't to the moon that every drop
> Of flower-held rain reflects and gazes on her!
> Her destiny is in the starry heavens,
> Theirs here upon the ground, and she doth set
> Leaving her shadow no more to delight them,
> And cometh ne'er again till they are fled.

Even a lily-of-the-valley becomes a jester with cap and bells, a symbol that motley is the whole world's wear.

Thus he follows beauty for ever through a maze, like some hidden Rosamond; he is himself

> the bird
> That can go up the labyrinthine winds
> Upon his pinions and pursues the summer.

He can turn to lucid grace even the image of ambiguity:

> I know not whether
> I see your meaning; if I do, it lies
> Upon the wordy wavelets of your voice
> Dim as the evening shadow in a brook
> When the least moon has silver on't no larger
> Than the pure white of Hebe's pinkish nail.

There seems nothing of which he cannot make music; even the streaks of rain seen in dark lines against the blue background of a showery sky become for his fingers the chords of a fantastic lyre. And yet with all his clever elaboration he can be agonizingly simple:

> They are both dead, and God has suffered it;

or again:

> Now I shall see him
> No more. All Hell is made of those two words.

Still, Beddoes is not often thus direct. He writes less of what he sees than of his thoughts in seeing it; what he describes is not so much like itself as like something else; and so a great part of both his strength and his sweetness will be found stored in his metaphors and similes. Like the Lady of Shalott, he watches the world remotely, in a strange mirror; like the Emperor Domitian, he walks, with terror about him, in a gallery of looking-glass.

Magic beauty and terror—as in his style and rhythm,

so in his mind and soul, these two seem to me his essential qualities, moving inseparably side by side. It might have been of him that Victor Hugo wrote:

> À de certains moments toutes les jeunes flores
> Dans la forêt
> Ont peur, et sur le front des blanches metaphores
> L'ombre apparaît.
> C'est qu'Horace ou Virgile ont vu soudain le spectre
> Noir se dresser;
> C'est que là-bas, derrière Amaryllis, Électre
> Vient de passer.

Only with Beddoes such moments are continual, and in his own pages, too, there are more shadows than there are men. This dualism moulds all his writing,

> As out of the same lump of sunny Nile
> Rises a purple-wingèd butterfly
> Or a cursed serpent crawls.

His most characteristic work becomes like a duet between a raven and a nightingale upon a tree in Hell. Now they alternate; now they blend together, as in that lovely picture of a Love who is also Death; a thin, pale Cupid with ragged wings and, for his dart, a frozen Zephyr,

> Gilt with the influence of an adverse star.
> Such was his weapon, and he traced with it,
> Upon the waters of my thoughts, these words:
> "I am the death of flowers and nightingales,
> Of small-lipped babes, that give their souls to summer
> To make a perfumed day with: I shall come,
> A death no larger than a sigh to thee,
> Upon a sunset hour." And so he passed
> Into the place where faded rainbows are,
> Dying along the distance of my mind.

At times, again, this duet becomes a duel; and just as in real life "he could be delightful if he chose" (said Mrs Procter), "but, oh, he chose so seldom", so in his letters the sardonic side of him will sneer at some pathetic passage just added to a play, and in his verse his raven will croak derision at his nightingale:

> I'll not be a fool like the nightingale
> Who sits up till midnight without any ale,
> Making a noise with his nose.

Thus at war within, he spared neither his country, nor his contemporaries, nor himself—poor dramatist ironically denuded of dramatic gift! But he was too hard on his own work. It is difficult to read through. I have done so twice, and never shall again. But I return with ever fresh astonishment to his fragments. The unfinished traceries, the ruined aisles of this gaunt sham-Gothic cathedral that he left half-built and roofless to the scorn of Time, will outlast many a neater and more finished edifice; saved by the almost unearthly perfectness of here a carved line and there a sculptured monster, and by the strange owl-light of its atmosphere in which Death's Jester wandered to his early and disastrous end. There is often more quintessential poetry, I feel, in three lines of his than in as many pages of other poets not without repute. Only wreckage remains of him; but enough to sustain his memory in that sea of Eternity into which he heard Time's river falling, himself so soon to fall.

Note.—I should like to add that Mr C. H. Wilkinson of Worcester College, Oxford, to whose kindness I owe a communication on the subject, regards Gosse's story of Browning's horror for the Beddoes MSS as an unconscious invention in Gosse's later memories. Browning's letter to Gosse inviting him to come and see the papers is extant, and quite calm in tone. The question is a difficult one and not important; it seems clear that Gosse exaggerated; but that he completely invented his story, even unconsciously or through misunderstanding, I find a little hard to believe.

I also owe Mr Wilkinson the correction (from the MS) "drink my health", for Gosse's "drink my death", on p. 35.

LETTERS

To BRYAN WALLER PROCTER

Milan, June 8th [*1824*]

*   *   *

And what else have I seen? A beautiful and far-famed insect—do not mistake, I mean neither the Emperor, nor the King of Sardinia, but a much finer specimen—the firefly. Their bright light is evanescent, and alternates with the darkness, as if the swift wheeling of the earth struck fire out of the black atmosphere; as if the winds were being set upon this planetary grindstone, and gave out such momentary sparks from their edges. Their silence is more striking than their flashes, for sudden phenomena are almost invariably attended with some noise, but these little jewels dart along the dark as softly as butterflies. For their light, it is not nearly so beautiful and poetical as our still companion of the dew—the glow-worm with his drop of moonlight. If you see or write to Kelsall, remember me to him; and excuse my neglect in not writing to him before I left England by the plea of hurry, which is true. To-night at twelve I leave Milan, and shall be at Florence on Saturday long before this letter tastes the atmosphere (*pardonnez*, I mean the smoke) of London.

There and here,

Yours truly,

T. L. BEDDOES

If you see Mrs Shelley, ask her to remember me, and tell her that I am as anxious to change countries with her as she can be. If I could be of any use in bringing the portrait, etc., it would be a proud task, but most likely I only flash over Florence; entering on the flood of the stars, and departing with their ebb.

To THOMAS FORBES KELSALL

6 Devereux C^t Temple Bar. [*Postmark Au: 25 1824*]

*   *   *

The disappearance of Shelley from the world, seems, like the tropical setting of that luminary (*aside* I hate that word) to which his poetical genius can alone be compared with reference to the companions of his day, to have been followed by instant darkness and owl-season; whether the vociferous Darley is to be the comet, or tender fullfaced L. E. L. the milk-and-watery moon of our darkness, are questions for the astrologers: if I were the literary weather-guesser for 1825 I would safely prognosticate fog, rain, blight in due succession for it's dullard months—

*   *   *

P.S. Shelley's book—This is a ghost indeed, and one who will answer to our demand for hidden treasure. The Dirge for the Year—That Indian Fragment—The boat on the Serchio and the Letter—with Music are to me the best of the new things and perfectly worthy of the mind which produced them. The translation of Mercury's hymn too; though questionable as to the fidelity of it's tone, is delightfully easy—

What would he not have done if ten years more, that will be wasted upon the lives of unprofitable knaves and fools, had been given to him. Was it that more of the beautiful and good, than Nature could spare to one, was incarnate in him, and that it was necessary to resume it for distribution through the external and internal worlds? How many springs will blossom with his thoughts—how many fair and glorious creations be born of his one extinction!

To THOMAS FORBES KELSALL

[*March the twenty fifth 1825*]

*   *   *

All that one hears of Schiller inclines one to admire him much more than his fat, leather-chopped, fish-eyed rival[1] with the mock star of Vonity on his padded coat. I have read that fellow's Tasso wʰ is a disgraceful apology for the conduct of the Duke of Ferrara, & represents poor Torquato, who was no great wit I fear, as an absolute spoiled poetic madman, a sort of Italian Tom Campbell—as touchy as tinder and as valuable. This was bound in a volume with his Iphigenie in Tauris, a poem faultlessly delightful, unless it be a fault that instead of being an imitation of Euripides it is a victory over him. I never felt so much disgust or much more admiration for any poet than for this Goëthe, as I read thro' it—& I believe every one who reads all his works must have this double feeling of contempt

[1] Goethe.

of & delight in him—both nearly measureless—but he has no principle; in thinking of Schiller you have more to admire than the paper he has written on.

The metrical translation I was rash enough to speak about stands thus—

Nibelungen-lied (German)   ...   ...   9965 lines.
Translated   120   ,,

you see why I don't send it. It is waiting to be finished —meantime I have abandoned my last new act—& begun the 3rd of that wʰ I was writing at Southton. I believe I may make an end of one or two in this way—

Be so good as to read—(if you can or do intend it) with a pencil in your hand & scratch all that is more particularly detestable & bad than ye rest.

Yours

T. L. B.

*   *   *

I will do the last man[1] before I die but it is a subject I save up for a time when I have more knowledge, a freer pencil, a little menschen-lehre, a command of harmony & an accumulation of picturesque ideas & dramatic characters, fit for the theme. Meantime let Tom Campbell rule his roast & mortify the ghost of Sternhold—it is a subject for Michael Angelo not for the painter of Admiral Granby on the sign-post. Did I tell ye, I had a very dull interview with that dealer

---

[1] *The Last Man*, one of the many plays planned by Beddoes.

in broken English, Dr Spurzheim, the ambassador from Golgotha? he is a strange breeches-full of mankind & seems inclined to the asinine.

*   *   *

To THOMAS FORBES KELSALL

Pemb Coll Oxford Wednesday [*Postmark 8 Ju: 1825*]

*   *   *

I do not intend to finish that 2nd Brother you saw but am thinking of a very Gothic-styled tragedy for w^h I have a jewel of a name—
DEATH'S JESTBOOK—of course no one will ever read it—Mr Milman (our poetry professor) has made me quite unfashionable here by denouncing me, as one of a "villainous school". I wish him another son—

*   *   *

To THOMAS FORBES KELSALL

Hamburg Tuesday. 19. July 1825

My dear Kelsall,—und mein lieber herr Thomas,— If you will take the sails of the Harwich packet, walk across the German Ocean, trot up the Elbe, & turn into the Roman Emperor at Hamburg be so good as to enquire for mein Herr T. L. B. No. 12 up two pair of stairs, & you will find him sitting on a horsehair sofa, looking over the Elbe with his meerschaum at his side full of Grave & abundantly prosaic.

Tomorrow, according to the prophecies of the diligence he will set out for Hanovver (we Germans (here a puff.) always spell it with 2 v's) & by the end of this week mein Herr Thomas will probably be a Dr of the university of Göttingen. What his intentions further may be I cannot say precisely as you & I between ourselves recollect that he is not altogether endued with the polar virtue of perseverance, & that the needle with w^h he embroiders his cloth of life has not been rubbed with the magnet of steady determination. I rather think however that he will return to England with a rather quaint and unintelligible tragedy, which will set all critical pens nib upwards, à la fretful porcupine.

When he embarked from Harwich & observed that his only companions were two Oxford men, professors of *genteel larking*, without the depth, vivacity or heartiness w^h is necessary to render such people tolerable, he instantly drew his shell over him, & remained impenetrably proud & silent every wave of the way, dropping now and then a little venom into the mixture of conversation to make it effervesce.

Hamburg, where he now is, poor young man, is a new brick-built town, a fit place to embellish the ugly genius of the broad flat-sided muddy Elbe—The very churches of brick & emetical unto the eye—The people honest and civil, & God fill their purse for it, no custom house no passport required—but then the women are of a coarse quality—there are no pictures no sculpture & if one meets more upright & manly forms in life, than in Italy, yet you seek in vain paintings superior to signs or sculpture beyond a tobacco-stopper.

Herr Procter, the Boet as George the Second says,

will tell you what a confusion was caused by your hoaxing letter to a B.A. of Pemb. Coll. Oxon—what a scrawl it ilicited (*sic*) from his drowsy quill & how *underlined* was the reply. Now leb wohl—for the post leaves us soon.

Fahrend oder reitend
sein

DER GENIUS VON T. L. B.

To THOMAS FORBES KELSALL

Cassel. Septr 29 [*1825*]

*   *   *

Blumenbach who is my best friend among the professors, is I fancy of the first rank as mineralogist, phisologian, geologist, botanist, natural historian & physician, over and above which he possesses an exuberant fancy & a flow of wit w^h is anything but German; indeed I suspect that he is the first living writer in Deutschland, for a nearer acquaintance with Goethe has inclined me to rate him much lower than I had anticipated; out of his works w^h fill pretty fatly some 30 vols—not like Mr Colburn's in capacity of page—3 at most contain what is really good. As a poet is he inferior to his late lordship[1] and in the novel line somewhere about Mackenzie. The hasty Germans have betrayed their literature & delivered it to the enemy by exalting him to the supreme godship thereof —but ere his bones are cool probably they will pull down his statue from it's high pinnacle on the poetic

[1] Byron.

temple and make it a step to the high altar of some new
pen-deity—

*   *   *

To THOMAS FORBES KELSALL

[*Postmark Göttingen Decr 4 1825*] *Sunday*
My dear Kelsall,

Up at 5 Anatomical reading till 6—translation from
English into German till 7—Prepare for Blumenbach's
lecture on comp. Anat^y & breakfast till 8—Blumen-
bach's lecture till 9—Stromeyer's lecture on Chemistry
till 10. 10 to ½ p. 12 Practical Zootomy—½ p. 12 to 1
English into German or German literary reading with
a pipe—1 to 2 Anatomical lecture. 2 to 3 anatomical
reading. 3 to 4 Osteology. 4 to 5 Lecture in German
language. 5 to 6 dinner and *light* reading in Zootomy
Chem. or Anat^y. 6 to 7—this hour is very often
wasted in a visit sometimes Anatomical reading till 8.
Then coffee and read Greek till 10. 10 to 11. write a
little Death's Jest book w^h is a horrible waste of time,
but one must now & then throw away the dregs of
the day; read Latin sometimes or even continue the
Anatomy—and at 11 go to bed.

I give you this account of my week-day occupations
that you may collect from it how small a portion of
time I can save for correspondence &^c. A few words
in answer to your last letter. I will frankly confess
to you that I have lost much if not all of my ambition
to become poetically distinguished: & I do NOT think
with Wordsworth that a man may dedicate himself
entirely or even in great part to the cultivation of that

part of literature, unless he possesses far greater powers of imagination &ᶜ than even W. himself, and, (I need not add;) ergo, than I do; or bodily ill-health or mental weakˢ prevents him from pursuing to any good purpose studies in useful sciences.

At the same time I think you will not fear that I shall become at any time a bare & barren man of science, such as are so abundant & so appallingly ignorant on this side of Chemistry or Anatomy. Again, even as a dramatist, I cannot help thinking that the study of anatʸ, phisol-psych: & anthropology applied to and illustrated by history, biography and works of imagination is that wʰ is most likely to assist one in producing correct and masterly delineations of the passions: great light wᵈ be thrown on Shakespeare by the commentaries of a person so educated. The studies then of the dramatist & physician are closely, almost inseparably, allied; the application alone is different; but is it impossible for the same man to combine these two professions in some degree at least?

*   *   *

And now I will end this unnecessary subject, by telling you that Death's Jest-book goes on like the tortoise slow & sure; I think it will be entertaining, very unamiable, & utterly unpopular. Very likely it may be finished in the spring or summer;

*   *   *

I feel myself in a measure alone in the world & likely to remain so, for from the experiments I have made I fear I am a non-conductor of friendship, a

not-very-likeable person so that I must make sure of
my own respect & occupy that part of the brain w^h
should be employed in imaginative attachments in the
pursuit of immaterial & unchanging good.

*   *   *

To BRYAN WALLER PROCTER

> [*Postmarks "Göttingen 7 Mar" "F.P.O. Mr 13 1826"*]
> *"Direct An Herrn Beddoes bey Eysel*
> *77 Weender Strasse Göttingen Hannover"*

TO-DAY a truant from the odd old bones
And winds of flesh, which, as tamed rocks and stones
Piled cavernously make his body's dwelling,
Have housed man's soul: there, where time's billows
    swelling
Make a deep ghostly and invisible sea
Of melted worlds, antidiluvially
Upon the sand of ever-crumbling hours
God-founded, stands the castle, all it's towers
With veiny tendrils ivied: this bright day
I leave its chambers, and with oars away
Seek some enchanted island where to play.
And what do you, that in the enchantment dwell
And should be raving ever, a wild swell
Of passionate life rolling about the world
Now sunsucked to the clouds, dashed on the curled
Leafhidden daisies; an incarnate storm
Letting the sun through on the meadows yellow;
Or anything except that earthy fellow,

That wise dog's brother, man? O shame to tell!
Make tea in Circe's cup, boil the cool well,
The well Pierian, which no bird dare sip
But nightingales! There let them kettles dip
Who write their simpering sonnets to it's song
And walk on sundays in Parnassus park.
Take thy example from the sunny lark,
Throw off the mantle which conceals the soul,
The many-citied world, and seek thy goal
Straight as a starbeam falls. Creep not nor climb
As they who place their topmost of sublime
On some peak of this planet pitifully,
Dart eaglewise with open wings and fly,
Until you meet the gods. Thus council[1] I
The men who can, but tremble to be great;
Cursed be the fool who taught to hesitate
And to regret: time lost most bitterly.
And thus I write and I dare write to thee,
Fearing that still, as you were wont to do,
You feed and fear some asinine Review.
Let Juggernaut roll on, and we, whose sires
Blooded his wheels and prayed around his fires,
Laugh at the leaden ass in the God's skin.
Example follows precept. I have been
Giving some negro minutes of the night
Freed from the slavery of my ruling spright,
Anatomy the grim, to a new story
In whose satiric pathos we will glory.
In it Despair has married wildest Mirth
And to their wedding-banquet all the earth

[1] *Sic.*

Is bade to bring its enmities and loves
Triumphs and horrors: you shall see the doves
Billing with quiet joy and all the while
Their nest's the skull of some old King of Nile:
But he who fills the cups and makes the jest,
Pipes to the dancers, is the fool o' the feast—
Who's he? I've dug him up and decked him trim
And made a mock, a fool, a slave of him
Who was the planet's tyrant: dotard Death:
Man's hate and dread: not with a stoical breath
To meet him like Augustus standing up,
Nor with grave saws to season the cold cup
Like the philosopher, nor yet to hail
His coming with a verse or jesting tale,
As Adrian did and More: but of his night,
His moony ghostliness and silent might
To rob him, to uncypress him i' the light,
To unmask all his secrets; make him play
Momus o'er wine by torchlight; is the way
To conquer him and kill; and from the day
Spurned, hissed and hooted send him back again
An unmasked braggart to his bankrupt den.
For death is more "a jest" than life; you see
Contempt grows quick from familiarity.
I owe this wisdom to Anatomy—
Your muse is younger in her soul than mine,—
O feed her still on woman's smiles and wine,
And give the world a tender song once more,
For all the good can love and can adore
What's human, fair and gentle. Few, I know,
Can bear to sit at my board when I show

The wretchedness and folly of man's all
And laugh myself right heartily. Your call
Is higher and more human: I will do
Unsociably my part & still be true
To my own soul: but e'er admire you
And own that you have nature's kindest trust
Her weak and dear to nourish,—that I must.
Then fare, as you deserve it, well, and live
In the calm feelings you to others give.

There, Mr B. C., is your small doggrell; a punishment, tolerably severe, for your delay in answering my letter; pray be as lazy again and you shall have a "double only" of German hexameters in the Klopstock style.

*   *   *

To THOMAS FORBES KELSALL

April 1. A bad omen! [*1826*]

My dear Kelsall,

If you had received all the letters which I had wished to write to you, you would have little to complain on the score of slack correspondency, but really we people in Germany have as little to say as we people in England and my thoughts all run on points very uninteresting to you—i.e. on entrails and blood-vessels; except a few which every now and then assume an Iambic form towards the never-ending Jestbook; it lies like a snow ball and I give it a kick every now & then out of mere scorn and ill-humour. the 4th act & I may say the 5th are more than half done, so that at last it will be a perfect mouse: but such doggeril—ask Procter else whom I lately visited with a rhyming punishment for his correspondential sin.

*   *   *

You'd be quite delighted to see how I disguise myself here: no human being w^d imagine that I was anything but the most stoical, prosaic, dull anatomist: I almost outwork the laborious Lauerkrauss—and to tell you truly I begin to prefer Anatomy &c to poetry, I mean to my own, & practically besides I never c^d have been the real thing as a writer: there *shall* be no more accurate physiologist & dissector.

*   *   *

Benecke who taught Coleridge German here, says that he has a very superficial knowledge of it. From what I know of Kant, i.e. his Anthropology—a very sensible acute man-of-the-world book—I suspect C. has never read him, at all events he has given the English a totally absurd opinion of him. Thank you for the box, because it never came. Do what you will or can with the other things: you are very welcome to Schiller to enrich your upper shelves: I shall not read him ever again. Ask me about poets &c? talk of Anatomists & I'll tell you something. I have left off reading Parnassian foolery. I can bear a satire still tho' and write one as Jest-book shall show. Tell me about the last Man.[1]

*   *   *

Why did you send me the Cenci? I open my own page, & see at once what damned trash it all is. No

---

[1] Beddoes' play, *The Last Man.*

truth or feeling. How the deuce do you, a third &
disinterested person, manage to tolerate it? I thank
heaven that I am sitting down pretty steadily to
medical studies. Labour then can do almost all.

*   *   *

To THOMAS FORBES KELSALL

Göttingen [*Postmark Oct: 5 1826*]

*   *   *

Goethe is preparing a new edition of his rhymed &
prosy commissions. xxxx. vols for 10 dollars who'll
buy who'll buy? They are as cheap as oysters if not
so swallowable.

In the neighbourhood of Göttingen is a slightly
Chalybeate spring & a little inn with a tea garden
whither students & Philistines (i.e. townsmen who are
not students) resort on sundays to dance & ride on
the Merry-go-round, an instrument of pleasure which
is always to be found on such places, and is much
ridden by the German students, perhaps because it as
well as waltzing produces mechanically the same
effects as the weekday hobby-horse, the philosophy of
Schelling &c, doth physically i.e. a giddiness & con-
fusion of the brain.

Behind this Terpsicorean τέμενος rises a woody
rocky eminence on which stands a fair high tower &
some old mossy and ivy-hugged walls, the remains of
an old castle called the Plesse: the date of the tower
is said to be 963: if this be true it may have earned a
citizenship among the semi-eternal stony populace of

the planet: at all events it will be older than some hills
which pretend to be natural & carry trees and houses—
e.g. Monte Nuovo.

On this hill & in the holes and vaults of the old
building resides a celebrated reptile, which we have
not in England—the salamander. He is to a lizard
what a toad is to a frog, slow, fat & wrinkled—of a
mottled black & yellow; it is true that under his skin
one finds a thick layer of a viscid milky fluid of a
peculiar not disagreeable smell which the beast has the
power of ejecting when irritated & by this means might
for a short time resist the power of fire.

Where the vulgar fable has its origin I am altogether
ignorant, I believe it comes from the middle ages;
from the monkish writers of natural history perhaps—
& they might have had a spite against the poor
amphibium, because he is unorthodox enough to live
a long while after you have removed his stomach &
intestines—& therefore condemned him to the flames
for impiety against the belly gods ’Αδηφαγία &
’Ακρατοπότης. The servants at the altar of these
thundering deities (v. Euripides *Cyclops* 327) may ad-
duce physiological authority for the immateriality of
their adored Paunch. J. Baptista van Helmont placed
the soul, which he nick-named Archaeus, in the
stomach & whatever the clergy know more about the
spirit in question I do not think they are inclined to
let the cat out of the bag. This is a pleasant doctrine
for aldermen and Kings, the dimensions of the soul
perhaps corresponding with the size of its habitation:
only they must beware of purges, it would be a mishap

to leave one's soul in a close-stool-pan like George
the 2nd.   *   *   *

I

"Come with me, thou gentle maid,
The stars are strong and make a shade
Of yew across your mother's tomb.
Leave your chamber's vineleaved gloom
Leave your harpstrings, loved one,
'Tis our hour," the robber said.
"Yonder comes the goblin's sun,
For when men are still in bed
Day begins with the old dead.
Leave your flowers so dewed with weeping
And our fev'rish baby sleeping;
Come to me, thou gentle maid,
'Tis our hour," the robber said.

II

To the wood whose shade is night
Went they in the owl's moonlight;
As they passed, the common wild
Like a murderous jester smiled
Dimpled twice with Nettly graves.
You may mark her garment white
In the night wind how it waves:
The night wind to the churchyard flew
And whispered underneath the yew,
"Mother Churchyard, in my breath
I've a lady's sigh of death."
"Sleep thou there, thou robber's wife,"
Said he, clasping his wet knife.

To THOMAS FORBES KELSALL

[*Postmark Göttingen 20 April: 1827*]

*   *   *

I am now already so thoroughly penetrated with the conviction of the absurdity & unsatisfactory nature of human life that I search with avidity for every shadow of a proof or probability of an after-existence both in the material & immaterial nature of man. Those people, perhaps they are few, are greatly to be envied who believe honestly and from conviction in the Xtian doctrines: but really in the New T. it is difficult to scrape together hints for a doctrine of immortality— Man appears to have found out this secret for himself & it is certainly the best part of all religion and philosophy, the only truth worth demonstrating: an anxious Question full of hope & fear & promise, for wh. Nature appears to have appointed one solution— Death. In times of revolution & business, and even now, the man who can lay much value in the society, praise, or glory of his fellows may forget, and he who is of a callous phlegmatic constitution may never find, the dreadful importance of the doubt. I am haunted for ever by it; & what but an after-life can satisfy the claims of the oppressed in nature, satiate endless & admirable love & humanity & quench the greediness of the spirit for existence?

*   *   *

To THOMAS FORBES KELSALL

A Tuesday in Oct. Göttingen
[Postmark 21 Oct. 1827]

*　　*　　*

I can really send you nothing of my own, I have a
pretty good deal in fragments which I want to cement
together and make a play of—among them is the last
Man. They will go all into the Jest-book—or the Fool's
Tragedy—the historical nucleus of which is an isolated
and rather disputed fact, that Duke Boleslaus of
Münsterberg in Silesia was killed by his court fool
A.D. 1377. but that is the least important part of the
whole fable. I have dead game in great quantities but
when or how it will be finished Æsculapius alone
knows: I will give you a song out of it wʰ seems to
me bad—but my English vocabulary is growing daily
more meagre, and I have neither much time nor much
inclination to keep up my poetical style by perusing
our writers: I am becoming daily more obtuse for
such impressions and rather read a new book on
anatomy than a new poem English or German.

Yet let me assure you that your idea of my merits
as a writer is extravagantly surpassing my real worth:
I wᵈ really not give a shilling for anything I have
written, nor sixpence for anything I am likely to write.
I am essentially unpoetical in character, habits & ways
of thinking: and nothing but the desperate hunger for
distinction so common to young gentlemen at the
Univʸ, ever set me upon rhyming. If I had possessed
the conviction that I could by any means become an

important or great dramatic writer I would have never swerved from the path to reputation: but seeing that others who had devoted their lives to literature, such as Coleridge and Wordsworth, men beyond a question of far higher originality and incomparably superior poetical feeling and Genius, had done so little, you must give me leave to persevere in my preference of Apollo's pill box to his lyre, & should congratulate me on having chosen Göttingen instead of Grub street for my abode—

Indeed all young verse-grinders ought to be as candid and give way to the really inspired. What would have been my confusion & dismay, if I had set up as a poet, and later in my career anything real and great had start up amongst us & like a real devil in a play frightened into despair & futerity (*sic*) the miserable masked wretches who mocked his majesty.

These are my real and good reasons for having at last rendered myself up to the study of a reputable profession in which the desire of being useful may at least excuse me altho I may be unequal to the attempt to become a master in it; & I assure you that the approbation which you have pleased to bestow upon a very sad boyish affair, that same Brides Tr: which I w^d not even be condemned to read through for any consideration, appears to me a remarkable & incomprehensible solecism of your otherwise sound literary judgement.

*   *   *

To THOMAS FORBES KELSALL

[Postmark Göttingen 27 Feby 1829]

*   *   *

My cursed fellows in the jestbook would palaver immeasurably & I could not prevent them. Another time it shall be better, that is to say if the people make it worth my while to write again. For if this affair excites no notice I think I may conclude that I am no writer for the time & generation, and we all know that posterity will have their own people to talk about.

You are, I think disinclined to the stage: now I confess that I think this is the highest aim of the dramatist, and should be very desirous to get on it. To look down on it is a piece of impertinence as long as one chooses to write in the form of a play, and is generally the result of a consciousness of one's own inability to produce anything striking & affecting in that way. Shakespeare wrote only for it, Ld B. despised it, or rather affected this as well as every other passion, which is the secret of his style in poetry & life.

*   *   *

To BRYAN WALLER PROCTER

19th April, 1829

*   *   *

For of the three classes of defects which you mention—obscurity, conceits, and mysticism,—I am afraid I am blind to the first and last, as I may be supposed to have associated a certain train of ideas to a certain mode of expressing them, and my four German years may have a little impaired my English style; and to the second I am, alas! a little partial, for Cowley was the first poetical writer whom I learned to understand. I will, then, do my best for the Play this summer; in the autumn I return to London, and then we will see what can be done. I confess to being idle and careless enough in these matters, for one reason, because I often very shrewdly suspect that I have no real poetical call.

I would write more songs if I could, but I can't manage rhyme well or easily. I very seldom get a glimpse of the right sort of idea in the right light for a song; and eleven out of the dozen are always good for nothing. If I could rhyme well and order complicated verse harmoniously, I would try odes; but it's too difficult.

*   *   *

To THOMAS FORBES KELSALL

April the last^e Göttingen '29 [*1829*]

*   *   *

Here is something of old Walther von der Vogelweide who wrote in the earlier part of the 13th century, but in his old German it is infinitely better.

> Under the lime-tree on the daisied ground
>   Two that I know of made this bed.
> There you may see heaped and scattered round
>   Grass and blossoms broken and shed,
>   All in a thicket down in the dale;
> Tandaradei—sweetly sang the nightingale.

Ere I set foot in the meadow already
  Some one was waiting for somebody;
There was a meeting—Oh! gracious lady,
  There is no pleasure again for me.
    Thousands of kisses there he took,
Tandaradei—see my lips, how red they look.
Leaf and blossom he had pulled and piled
  For a couch, a green one, soft and high;
And many a one hath gazed and smiled
  Passing the bower and pressed grass by:
    And the roses crushed hath seen,
Tandaradei, where I laid my head between;
In this love-passage if any one had been there,
  How sad and shamed should I be;
But what were we a-doing alone among the green there
  No soul shall ever know except my love and me,
    And the little nightingale
Tandaradei—she, I wot, will tell no tale.

       *   *   *

To THOMAS FORBES KELSALL

                  Wurzburg 2 District No 110
                  [*Postmark 19 July 1830*]

My dear Kelsall,—Your letter finds me at leizure
(*sic*) (excuse all misspellings, my mother tongue begins
to fade away in my memory and I was just going to
write this word analogically like pleasure) and I will
reply to, though perhaps not answer it. All about the
play annoys me because I have utterly neglected it
and feel not the least inclination to take any further

trouble in the matter: however perhaps I may try this season; it cannot be printed this summer, and in autumn perhaps something may be done. This in-difference is of itself almost enough to convince me that my nature is not that of one who is destined to atchieve anything very important in this department of literature; another is a sort of very moderate some-what contemptuous respect for the profession of a mere poet in our inky age.

You will conceive that such a feeling accords well with, and perhaps results from, a high delight in first-rate creators and illustrators of the creation as Æschylus, Shak. &c and a cordial esteem for those who, as highly polished moderns, have united their art with other solid knowledge & science, or political activity— Camoens, Dante & lower down many French and English accomplished rhymers;—and now Goethe, Tieck &c.

In the third place a man must have an exclusive passion for his art, and all the obstinacy and self-denial wh: is combined with such a temperament, an un-conquerable and all-enduring will always working forwards to the only goal he knows; such a one must never think that there is any human employment so good (much less suspect that there may be not a few better,) so honourable for the exercise of his faculties, ambition, industry—and all those impolitic and hasty virtues which helped Icarus to buckle on his plumes and wh we have left sticking in the pages of Don Quixote.

I am even yet however seriously of the opinion that it is ornamental and honourable to every nation and generation of mankind if they cherish among their numbers men of cultivated imagination capable of producing new·and valuable works of art; and if I were soberly and mathematically convinced of my own genuineness (*inspiration* as the ancients w^d say) I might possibly, tho' I *won't promise*, find spirit and stability enough to give up my time to the cultivation of literature.

If dreams were dramatic calls as in the days or nights of Æschylus I might plead something too—He, according to Athenæus, sleeping in a vineyard, probably after acting a part in some Thespian satyric dialogue, had a vision of Bacchus descending to him and bidding him arise and write tragedies. The author of Agamemnon had a good right to relate such a nocturnal visit, if it had been paid to him, or even to invent it if a less divine nightmare had invited him to mount his hobby-horse. We will not ask how many have won in this or any other lottery and the number they saw in their slumbers. I in my bed in Wurzburg did dream that I bought in an old bookshop for a small moiety of copper money, a little old dirty, dogs-eared, well-thumbed book and thereon in great agitation and joy saw at the first glance into the dialogue ('twas a playbook,) that it contained half-a-dozen genuine and excellent unknown plays, wh: no one could have written whose name and nature was not W. S.

To return to reality I will say then that I will try to write over again this last unhappy play, tho' I have no appetite to the task, and then I w^d wish to have it printed with any other little things that you may have and think worth printer's ink because a second edition is not to be thought of, and any consequent poetical publication of mine very improbable.

It is good to be tolerable or intolerable in any other line, but Apollo defend us from brewing all our lives at a quintessential pot of the smallest ale Parnassian; such hope or memory is little soothing for any one whose mind is not quite as narrow as a column of eights and sixes.

I sometimes wish to devote myself exclusively to the study of anatomy & physiology in science, of languages, and dramatic poetry, and have nothing to hinder me except—unsteadiness and indolence: wh. renders it extremely probable if not absolutely certain that I shall never be anything above a very moderate dabbler in many waters: if another very different spirit does not come over me very very soon you will do well to give me up. Indifference grows upon us and that renders my case very desperate.

*   *   *

To THOMAS FORBES KELSALL

     Wurzburg 1 District No. 186
     [*Postmark 10 Jan 1831*]

*   *   *

And a play in four acts is a cripple. Either three or 5.

In the first the deed must be committed the consequences of wh employ the following: in the second a reaction attempted and a second seed sown for

ripening in the after-time: in the third, which needs
not to be the most powerful as I once thought, the
storm gathers, doubts rise, or the termination w^h ap-
pears to be at hand is intercepted by some bold and
unexpected invention; a new event, the developement
of a character hitherto obscure, a new resolve &^c gives
a new turn to the aspect of the future: in the fourth
all is consummated, the truth is cleared up, the final
determination taken, the step of Nemesis is heard: and
in the fifth the atonement follows.

The first, fourth and fifth must be most attractive
and interesting from the confliction of passions and
the events occasioned by them: the 2 is a pause for
retrospection, anticipation; in the third is rather the
struggle between the will of man and the moral law
of necessity w^h awaits inevitably his past actions—the
pivot of all tragedy.

*   *   *

Many things are quite absurd and destructive of all
poetry in arrangements w^h appear not of the slightest
consequence. I am convinced that playbills for instance
are very pernicious; one should never know the actors'
names and private circumstances, the spectators would
then be compelled to identify them with their dramatic
characters, the interest w^d be much purer and un-
divided, the illusion carried as far as it can & ought
to be—how can people enter deeply into the spirit
of a tragedy for instance—in comedy it is a matter of
less consequence—whose question is, how do you like
Kean to-night? Is not Claremont delightful in Rosen-
kranz? etc.—Othello & Richard & Rosenkranz are

here obliged to play Claremont & Kean instead of the reverse.

The actor on the other hand deprived of his private name & existence must feel more convinced of the reality of his 5-act life, would be liberated from the shackles of timidity & the temptations of individual vanity, w^d [grow] careless about his creditors & be unable to try & please the lady's as Mr —— with the handsome leg &c, wink to his friends in the pit &^c &^c. To whet curiosity and occasion astonishment is not the least important object of the dramatist; the actors might have learned from Scott that anonymous mysteriousness is one of the most effective arts for this purpose—A distant idea of the use of this concealment probably caused the custom observed in the announcement of a new play—principal characters by Messrs Doe & Roe—but the names of the people in the drama ought to be printed with the necessary key (father, son &^c) not those of the gentleman who lodges at the pastry cook's, wears the threadbare coat, &c.

The Greeks (from whom we can learn much if we understand their motives—) were in possession of this secret, and this is the real meaning of their masks, wh. have so much bothered the critics; and these were doubly useful, they deceived to a certain degree not only the spectator, but also the actor, with the semblance of an heroic and unknown person, and prevented the annoying familiarity of the people on the stage. Of course I do not wish to see these sort of masks on our stage—(our passionate drama renders them impossible —though it might be an interesting experiment to try them once in an adaptation of Agamemnon, the Bacchæ, Antigone or Electra—to conclude with the satyric Drama—the Cyclops:) it is only to be lamented that we have no other means of completely disguising our actors and making Richard, Hamlet, Macbeth as absolutely distinct and independent individuals as Œdipus & Orestes must have been—the Athenians wᵈ I am sure have pelted their fellow-citizen and neighbour as the pathetic hobbling, ulcerous Philoctetes off the stage with onions, only a conviction of his reality could have reconciled their frivolous imagination with him or subdued them to compassion—and Agamemnon or Hercules unmasked would have been saluted with their nicknames from all sides.

Othello's colour is a sort of mask, & this is a reason perhaps why Shak: has given him so much less ideal language and more simple household truth than his other characters, the whole play is barer of imagery than any other of his, except the musicians with their silver sound there is no conductor for laughter from the tragic characters; Sh: seems really to intend more illusion than elsewhere, & is not the purpose gained?

The witches, Peter & the nurse, the grave-diggers & Polonius, in a less degree Kent & Lear's Fool, are all more or less purposely destructive of the tragic illusion—give time to recover from the surprize wʰ the course of the events produce[s]: their good is that they give the hearer to understand that the poet is not absolutely in earnest with his deaths & horrors & leaves it to them to be affected with them or not as they think proper, and secondly, that the audience,

as well as everybody, is much less inclined to laugh
at & deride the gravity of a person, with whom his
wit & satire has compelled them to laugh—besides
that the change is grounded on the law of oscillation
w^h pervades all physical and moral nature—sleeping
and waking (merriment & tears), sin & repentance,
life & death, w^h all depend & are consequent on one
another.

So much for my dramaturgic ideas on playbills, I
do not know that any one else has fallen on them—
what do you think of them as theory? The pause
between the acts—w^h the Greeks and Sh: I believe
did not allow—is another dangerous innovation: the
thread of events is interrupted, one talks to one's
neighbour, hears news and forgets the fictitious in the
real events, the state of mind produced by the opening
is altered, and as soon as we are with difficulty brought
back to the track over w^h the poet w^d lead us another
interruption undoes all again. The actors in the mean-
time chat behind the scenes, Cordelia flirts with her
papa, Arthur makes King John a pigtail, Constance
comforts herself with a cup of tea, Juliet dances with
the dead Mercutio and all such things occur wh breed
familiarity & carelessness and damp the excited imagina-
tion, cool the ardour, of the players.

These & some other apparently trifling things have,
I am convinced, done the drama much more harm,
rendered it less poetical, and spoiled the audience &
performers, than the innocent dogs, & horses, who act
always better than the bipeds & w^h are as allowable
as painted houses &^c. Agamemnon's chariot was

drawn by real horses I doubt not, Shakespeare made a good use of his friend's dog who played Lance &c &c. I acknowledge that licences, patents, theatrical censure &c have been far more noxious; the stage must be as free as the press before anything very good comes again.

*   *   *

(Fragment) *To* REVELL PHILLIPS

Strasburg Septr 25th 1832

The absurdity of the King of Bavaria has cost me a good deal, as I was obliged to oppose every possible measure to the arbitrary illegality of his conduct, more for the sake of future objects of his petty royal malice than my own, of course in vain.

P.S. By the way I have taken an M.D. at Wurzburg but do not at present desire to make use of the title.

To THOMAS FORBES KELSALL

Zurich che₂ M. Waser Neustadt
[Postmark 9 March 1837]

My dear Kelsall,—I am preparing for the press, as the saying is, among other graver affairs, a volume[1] of prosaic poetry and poetical prose. It will contain half a dozen Tales, comic, tragic, and dithyrambic, satirical and semi-moral: perhaps half a hundred lyrical Jewsharpings in various styles and humours: and the stillborn D.J.B.[2] with critical and cacochymical re-

[1] To have been called *The Ivory Gate*, but never published.
[2] *Death's Jest-Book.*

marks on the European literature, in specie the hapless drama of our day.

I am not asinine enough to imagine that it will be any very great shakes, but what with a careless temper and the pleasant traunslunary moods I walk and row myself into upon the lakes and over the alps of Switzerland it will, I hope, turn out not quite the smallest ale brewed out with the water of the fountain of yᵉ horse's foot.

Now then, I write to beg you, as the saying is, to send me in a letter a copy of a certain scene and song wʰ you, being the possessor of the only existing MS. thereof, once proposed as an amelioration of one in D's J. B. This affair will be very much cut down, a good many faults corrected: a little new matter added to it: and the whole better arranged. But I can hardly consent to eradicate my crocodile song, wh, you know, B. C.[1] and all persons of proper feeling, as the saying is, strongly condemned. After all I only print it because it is written and can't be helped and really only for such readers as the pseudonymical lawyer mentioned, W. Savage L[andor]: yourself, etc.! (if there be yet a plural number left). G. D.[2] appears to me to have grown deuced grey, whether it be the greyness of dawn, of life's evening twilight, or of a nascent asinine metempsychosis I cannot distinguish at this distance.

*   *   *

[1] Barry Cornwall.   [2] George Darley.

To THOMAS FORBES KELSALL

[Postmark Zurich] May 15 [1837] the hills
covered with snow. Temperature + 6° R

*   *   *

You are desirous of knowing what my thoughts or
superstitions may be regarding things human, sub-
human, and superhuman: or you wish to learn my
habits, pursuits, and train of life. Now as you have
not me before you in the witness's box, you must
excuse my declining to answer directly to such ques-
tioning. I will not venture on a psychological self-
portraiture, fearing, and I believe with sufficient reason,
to be betrayed into affectation, dissimulation, or some
other alluring shape of lying. I believe that all auto-
biographical sketches are the result of mere vanity—
not excepting those of St Augustin & Rousseau—
falsehood in the mask & mantle of truth.

Half ashamed and half conscious of his mendacious
self-flattery the historian of his own deeds, or geo-
grapher of his own mind breaks out now and then
indignantly and revenges himself on his own weakness
by telling some very disagreeable truth of some other
person, and then re-established in his own good opinion
marches on cheerfully in the smooth path towards the
temple of his own immortality. Yet even here you see
I am indirectly lauding my own worship for not being
persuaded to laud my own worship. How sleek,
smooth-tongued, paradisical a deluder art thou, sweet
self-conceit! Let great men give their own thoughts

on their own thoughts: from such we can learn much:
but let the small deer hold jaw (*sic*) and remember
what the philosopher says, "fleas are not lobsters:
damn their souls."

*   *   *

To THOMAS FORBES KELSALL

Shiffnall Aug 11. 1846.

My dear Kelsall,—I have been in the native land of
the unicorn about a week and may remain 5 more:
I should wish to see and talk with you during my stay.
As you are the busy man I leave the arrangements to
your convenience. I had no time to visit Procter in
passing through London, but am told that he is ap-
pointed to a high office in the government of the
kingdom of yᵉ moon,[1] upon which, as a retired member
of the company of poets he was I suppose accustomed
to draw liberally.

*   *   *

To THOMAS FORBES KELSALL

Catherine St Grange Road Birkenhead
[Postmark Mr 10 1847]

*   *   *

It will give me great pleasure to confer with you,
but pray expect no addition to your experience from
the scenes of my existence; nothing can be more mono-
tonous, dull and obscure: the needy knife-grinder's

[1] Procter had been nominated a permanent Metropolitan
Commissioner of Lunacy.

adventures would have been oriental marvels and pantomimic mysteries in comparison. Prose of the leadenest drab dye has ever pursued your humble servant. But of that you will not doubt,—I believe I might have met with some success as a retailer of small coal, or a writer of long-bottomed tracts, but doubt of my aptitude for any higher literary or commercial occupation. But you will see—I believe I have all the dulness, if not the other qualities—of your British respectability.

*   *   *

To REVELL PHILLIPS

[January 26 1849]

My dear Phillips,—I am food for what I am good for—worms. I have made a will here which I desire to be respected, and add the donation of £20 to Dr Ecklin my physician.

W. Beddoes must have a case (50 bottles) of Champagne Moet 1847 growth to drink my health in.

Thanks for all kindness. Borrow the £200. You are a good & noble man & your children will have to look sharp to be like you.

Yours,

if my own,

ever,

T. L. B.

Love to Anna, Henry, the Beddoes of Longvill and Zoe and Emmeline King—also to Kelsall whom I beg

3-2

to look at my MSS. and print or not as he thinks fit.
I ought to have been among other things a good poet.
Life was too great a bore on one peg and that a bad
one. Buy for Dr Ecklin above mentioned [one of]
Reade's best stomach-pumps.

[This note, written in pencil, was found folded on the poet's
bosom, as he lay insensible after taking poison, in his bed in
the Town Hospital of Basel. He died at 10 P.M. the same night.]

THE BRIDES' TRAGEDY

HESPERUS loves FLORIBEL; but his friend ORLANDO, also in love
with her, has the father of HESPERUS arrested for debt and refuses to
release him unless HESPERUS weds his sister OLIVIA. HESPERUS yields,
and murders his old love to make room for the new. The deed is dis-
covered; he is condemned; and OLIVIA dies broken-hearted.

Act I

SCENE I. *A garden*

*   *   *

Flor. Jealous so soon, my Hesperus? Look then,
It is a bunch of flowers I pulled for you:
Here's the blue violet, like Pandora's eye,
When first it darkened with immortal life.
  Hesp. Sweet as thy lips. Fie on those taper fingers,
Have they been brushing the long grass aside
To drag the daisy from it's hiding-place,
Where it shuns light, the Danaë of flowers,
With gold up-hoarded on its virgin lap?
  Flor. And here's a treasure that I found by chance,
A lily of the valley; low it lay
Over a mossy mound, withered and weeping
As on a fairy's grave.
  Hesp.   Of all the posy
Give me the rose, though there's a tale of blood
Soiling its name. In elfin annals old
'Tis writ, how Zephyr, envious of his love,
(The love he bare to Summer, who since then
Has weeping visited the world;) once found
The baby Perfume cradled in a violet;

('Twas said the beauteous bantling was the child
Of a gay bee, that in his wantonness
Toyed with a pea-bud in a lady's garland;)
The felon winds, confederate with him,
Bound the sweet slumberer with golden chains,
Pulled from the wreathed laburnum, and together
Deep cast him in the bosom of a rose,
And fed the fettered wretch with dew and air.
At length his soul, that was a lover's sigh,
Waned from his body, and the guilty blossom
His heart's blood stained. The twilight-haunting gnat
His requiem whined, and harebells tolled his knell,
And still the bee, in pied velvet dight
With melancholy song, from flower to flower
Goes seeking his lost offspring.
   Flor.   Take it then,
In its green sheath. What guess you, Hesperus,
I dreamed last night? Indeed it makes me sad,
And yet I think you love me.

*   *   *

A vision of VENUS and CUPID.

Beneath them swarmed a bustling mob of Loves,
Tending the sparrow stud, or with bees' wings
Imping their arrows. Here stood one alone,
Blowing a pyre of blazing lovers' hearts
With bellows full of absence-caused sighs:
Near him his work-mate mended broken vows
With dangerous gold, or strung soft rhymes together
Upon a lady's tress. Some swelled their cheeks,

Like curling rose-leaves, or the red wine's bubbles,
In petulant debate, gallantly tilting
Astride their darts. And one there was alone
Who with wet downcast eyelids threw aside
The remnants of a broken heart, and looked
Into my face and bid me 'ware of love,
Of fickleness, and woe, and mad despair.

*   *   *

Act I

SCENE II
*   *

Claudio. Now by the patches on the cheek of the moon,
(Is't not a pretty oath?) a good romance;
We'll have 't in ballad metre, with a burthen
Of sighs, how one bright glance of a brown damsel
Lit up the tinder of Orlando's heart
In a hot blaze.
Orlando.   Enough to kindle up
An altar in my breast! 'Twas but a moment,
And yet I would not sell that grain of time
For thy eternity of heartlessness.
Claudio. Well, well. I can bear a nonsense from a lover;
Oh, I've been mad threescore and eighteen times
And three quarters; written twenty yards, two nails,
An inch and a quarter, cloth measure, of sonnets;
Wasted as much salt water as would pickle
Leviathan, and sighed enough to set up
Another wind;——
Orlando.   Claudio, I pray thee, leave me;
I relish not this mockery.
Claudio.   Good sir, attend

To my experience. You've no stock as yet
To set up lover: get yourself a pistol
Without a touch-hole, or at least remember,
If it be whole, to load it with wet powder;
I've known a popgun, well applied, or even
The flying of a cork, give reputation
To courage and despair. A gross of garters,
Warranted rotten, will be found convenient.

*   *   *

Act II

SCENE I

*   *

SONG
A ho! A ho!
Love's horn doth blow,
And he will out a-hawking go.
His shafts are light as beauty's sighs,
And bright as midnight's brightest eyes,
And round his starry way
The swan-winged horses of the skies,
With summer's music in their manes,
Curve their fair necks to zephyr's reins,
And urge their graceful play.

A ho! A ho!
Love's horn doth blow,
And he will out a-hawking go.
The sparrows flutter round his wrist,
The feathery thieves that Venus kissed
And taught their morning song;

The linnets seek the airy list,
And swallows too, small pets of Spring,
Beat back the gale with swifter wing,
    And dart and wheel along.

    A ho! A ho!
  Love's horn doth blow,
    And he will out a-hawking go.
Now woe to every gnat that skips
To filch the fruit of ladies' lips,
    His felon blood is shed;
And woe to flies, whose airy ships
On beauty cast their anchoring bite,
And bandit wasp, that naughty wight,
    Whose sting is slaughter-red.

   *   *   *

Aɛt II

SCENE II
  *   *

Enter HESPERUS

Hesp. Good morrow, Floribel.
Flor. Fair noon to Hesperus; I knew a youth,
In days of yore, would quarrel with a lark,
If with its joyous matins it foreran
His early pipe beneath his mistress' window;
Those days are passed; alas! for gallantry.
  Hesp. Floribel!
  Flor.   Sir, d'ye know the gentleman?
Give him my benison and bid him sleep
Another hour, there's one that does not miss him.
  Hesp. Lady, I came to talk of other things,

To tell you all my secrets: must I wait
Until it fits your humour?

    Flor.   As you please:
(The worst of three bad suitors, and his name
Began with an H.)

    Hesp. Good morrow then, again.

    Flor.   Heaven help you, sir,
And so adieu.

    Hesp. Madam, you spoke; you said it, Floribel:
I never thought mine ears a curse before.
Did I not love thee? Say, have I not been
The kindest?

    Flor.   Yes indeed thou *hast* been. Now
A month is over. What would I not give
For those four sevens of days? But I have lived
    them,
And that's a bliss. You speak as if I'd lost
The little love you gave your poor one then.

    Hesp. And you as if you cared not for the loss.
Oh Floribel, you'll make me curse the chance
That fashioned this sad clay and made it man;
It had been happier as the senseless tree
That canopies your sleep. But Hesperus,
He's but the burthen of a scornful song
Of coquetry; beware, that song may end
In a death-groan.

    Flor. (*sings*).

           The knight he left the maid,
              That knight of fickleness,
           Her's was the blame he said,
              And his the deep distress.

If you are weary of poor Floribel,
Pray be not troubled; she can do without thee.
Oh Hesperus, come hither, I must weep;
Say, you will love me still, and I'll believe it,
When I forget my folly.

            *   *   *

A&t II

SCENE III
            *   *

Hesp. Then thou shalt be mine own; but not till death:
We'll let this life burn out, no matter how;
Though every sand be moistened with our tears,
And every day be rain-wet in our eyes;
Though thou shouldst wed some hateful avarice,
And I grow hoary with a daubed deceit,
A smiling treachery in woman's form,
Sad to the soul, heart-cankered and forlorn;
No matter, all no matter.
Though madness rule our thoughts, despair our hearts,
And misery live with us, and misery talk,
Our guest all day, our bed-fellow all night;
No matter, all no matter.
For when our souls are born then will we wed;
Our dust shall mix and grow into one stalk,
Our breaths shall make one perfume in one bud,
Our blushes meet each other in a rose,
Our sweeter voices swell some sky-bird's throat
With the same warbling, dwell in some soft pipe,
Or bubble up along some sainted spring's

Musical course, and in the mountain trees
Slumber our deeper tones, by tempests waked:
We will be music, spring, and all fair things,
The while our spirits make a sweeter union
Than melody and perfume in the air.
Wait then, if thou dost love me.
    Olivia.   Be it so;
You'll let me pray for death, if it will bring
Such joys as these? Though once I thought to live
A happy bride; but I must learn new feelings.
    Hesp. New feelings! Aye to watch the lagging clock,
And bless each moment as it parts from thee,
To court the blighting grasp of tardy age,
And search thy forehead for a silver tress
As for a most prized jewel.
    Olivia.   I cannot think
Of that cold bed diseases make for us,
That earthy sleep; oh! 'tis a dreadful thing.
    Hesp. The very air,
I thank it, (the same wild and busy air,
That numbers every syllable I speak,
In the same instant my lips shape its sound,
With the first lisps of him, who died before
The world began its story;) steals away
A little from my being;
And at each slightest tremour of a leaf
My hearse moves one step nearer. Joy, my love!
We're nearer to our bridal sheets of lead
Than when your brother left us here just now,
By twenty minutes' talk.
    Olivia.   It is not good

Thus to spurn life, the precious gift of heaven
And watch the coming light of dissolution
With such a desperate hope. Can we not love
In secret, and be happy in our thoughts,
Till in devotion's train, th' appointed hour
Lead us, with solemnly rejoicing hearts,
Unto our blessed end?

Hesp.   End! thou sayest.
And do those cherries ripen for the worms,
Those blue enchantments beam to light the tomb?
Was that articulate harmony Love uses
Because he seems both Love and Innocence
When he sings to it, that summer of sweet breath,
Created but to perish and so make
The dead's home loveliest?

Olivia. But what's to live without my Hesperus?
A life of dying. 'Tis to die each moment
In every several sense. To look despair,
Feel, taste, breathe, eat, be conscious of despair.
No, I'll be nothing rather.

Hesp.   Nothing but mine!
Thou flower of love, I'll wear thee in my bosom;
With thee the wrath of man will be no wrath,
Conscience and agony will smile like pleasure,
And sad remembrance lose its gloomy self
In rapturous expectation.

Olivia.   Let me look on thee;
Pray pardon me, mine eyes are very fools.

Hesp. Jewels of pity, azure stars of beauty
Which lost affection steers by; could I think
To dim your light with sorrow? Pardon me,

And I will serve you ever. Sweet, go in;
Somewhat I have to think on.

*   *   *

Act II

SCENE VI. *A suicide's grave*

ORLANDO *and* CLAUDIO

Clau. There is a plague in this night's breath, Orlando,
The dews fall black and blistering from yon cloud
Anchored above us; dost thou mark how all
The smokes of heaven avoid it and crowd on
Far from its fatal darkness? Some men say
That the great king of evil sends his spirits
In such a wingèd car, to stir ill minds
Up to an act of death.

Orl.   We may not think so,
For there's a fascination in bad deeds,
Oft pondered o'er, that draws us to endure them,
And then commit. Beware of thine own soul:
'Tis but one devil ever tempts a man,
And his name's *Self.* Know'st thou these rankling
    hemlocks?

Clau. I've seen the ugsome reptiles battening on them,
While healthy creatures sicken at the sight.

Orl. Five months ago they were an human heart
Beating in Hugo's breast. A parricide
Here sleeps, self-slaughtered. 'Twas a thing of grace,
In his early infancy; I've known him oft
Outstep his pathway, that he might not crush
The least small reptile. But there is a time

When goodness sleeps; it came, and vice was grafted
On his young thoughts, and grew, and flourished there:
Envenomed passions clustered round that prop;
A double fruit they bore; a double fruit of death.
  Clau. Enough, Orlando.
The imps of darkness listen, while we tell
A dead man's crimes. Even now I hear a stir,
As if the buried turned them in their shrouds
For mere unquiet. Home, it is the time
When the hoarse fowl, the carrier-bird of woe,
Brings fevers from the moon, and maddening dreams;
The hour's unholy, and who hath not sent
After the parted sun his orisons,
Falls 'neath the sway of evil.   [*Exeunt*

Aɕ III

SCENE III. *A wood*

Enter HUBERT *and a* Huntsman

  Hub. No answer to our shouts but mocking echo?
Where are our fellow huntsmen? Why, they vanished
Like mist before the sun, and left us here
Lost in the briary mazes.
  Hunts.   Shame on the rogues
For this their treatment. But look upwards, Hubert,
See what a mighty storm hangs right above us.
  Hub. The day is in its shroud while yet an infant;
And Night with giant strides stalks o'er the world,
Like a swart Cyclops, on its hideous front
One round, red, thunder-swollen eye ablaze.
  Hunts. Now mercy save the peril-stricken man,

Who 'mongst his shattered canvas sits aghast
On the last sinking plank alone, and sees
The congregated monsters of the deep
For his dead messmates warring, all save one
That leers upon him with a ravenous gaze
And whets its iron tusks just at his feet:
Yet little heeds his wide and tearless eye
That, or the thunder of the mountain flood
Which Destiny commissions with his doom;
Where the wild waters rush against the sky,
Far o'er the desolate plain, his star of hope
In mockery gleams, while Death is at his side.

*   *   *

Floribel.   Oh, my love,
Some spirit in thy sleep hath stolen thy body
And filled it to the brim with cruelty.

*   *   *

Act V

SCENE III

*   *

Olivia.   Violetta,
Dost thou regard my wish, perhaps the last?
     Viol. Oh! madam, can you doubt it? We have lived
Together ever since our little feet
Were guided on the path, and thence have shared
Habits and thoughts. Have I in all that time,
That long companionship, e'er thwarted thee?
Why dost thou ask me then? Indeed I know not
Thy wishes from my own, but to prefer them.

Then tell me what you will; if its performance
But occupy the portion of a minute,
'Twill be a happy one, for which I thank you.
   Olivia. Thine hand upon it; I believe thy promise.
When I am gone you must not weep for me,
But bring your books, your paintings, and your flowers,
And sit upon my grassy monument
In the dewy twilight, when they say souls come
Walking the palpable gross world of man,
And I will waft the sweetest odours o'er you;
I'll shower down acorn-cups of spicy rain
Upon your couch, and twine the boughs above;
Then, if you sing, I'll take up Echo's part,
And from a far-off bower give back the ends
Of some remembered airy melody;
Then, if you draw, I'll breathe upon the banks
And freshen up the flowers, and send the birds,
Stammering their madrigals, across your path;
Then, if you read, I'll tune the rivulets,
I'll teach the neighbouring shrubs to fan your temples,
And drive sad thoughts and fevers from your breast;
But, if you sleep, I'll watch your truant sense,
And meet it in the fairy-land of dreams
With my lap full of blessings; 'twill, methinks,
Be passing pleasant, so don't weep for me.

        *   *   *

DEATH'S JEST-BOOK:

OR THE FOOL'S TRAGEDY

Act I

SCENE I. *Port of Ancona*

Enter MANDRAKE *and* JOAN

Mandr. Am I a man of gingerbread that you should mould me to your liking? To have my way, in spite of your tongue and reason's teeth, tastes better than Hungary wine; and my heart beats in a honey-pot now I reject you and all sober sense: so tell my master, the doctor, he must seek another zany for his booth, a new wise merry Andrew. My jests are cracked, my coxcomb fallen, my bauble confiscated, my cap decapitated. Toll the bell; for oh! for oh! Jack Pudding is no more!

Joan. Wilt thou away from *me* then, sweet Mandrake? Wilt thou not marry me?

Mandr. Child, my studies must first be ended. Thou knowest I hunger after wisdom, as the red sea after ghosts: therefore will I travel awhile.

Joan. Whither, dainty Homunculus?

Mandr. Whither should a student in the black arts, a journeyman magician, a Rosicrucian? Where is our country? You heard the herald this morning thrice invite all christian folk to follow the brave knight, Sir Wolfram, to the shores of Egypt, and there help to free from bondage his noble fellow in arms, Duke Melveric, whom, on a pilgrimage to the Holy Sepulchre, wild pagans captured. There, Joan, in that Sphynx land found Raimund Lully those splinters of the philosopher's stone with which he made English Edward's gold. There dwell hoary magicians, who have given up their trade and live sociably as crocodiles on the banks of the Nile. There can one chat with mummies, in a pyramid, and breakfast on basilisk's eggs. Thither then, Homunculus Mandrake, son of the great Paracelsus; languish no more in the ignorance of these climes, but abroad with alembic and crucible, and weigh anchor for Egypt.

Enter ISBRAND

Isbr. Good morrow, brother Vanity! How? soul of a pickle-herring, body of a spagirical[1] toss-pot, doublet of motley, and mantle of pilgrim, how art thou transmuted! Wilt thou desert our brotherhood, fool sublimate? Shall the motley chapter no longer boast thee? Wilt thou forswear the order of the bell, and break thy vows to Momus? Have mercy on Wisdom and relent.

Mandr. Respect the grave and sober, I pray thee. To-morrow I know thee not. In truth, I mark that our noble faculty is in its last leaf. The dry rot of prudence hath eaten the ship of fools to dust; she is no more seaworthy. The world will see its ears in a glass no longer; so we are laid aside and shall soon be forgotten; for why should the feast of asses come but once a year, when all the days are foaled of one mother? O world, world! The gods and fairies left thee, for thou wert too wise; and now, thy Socratic[2]

---

[1] alchemical.   [2] *thou*, previous editions.

star, thy demon, the great Pan, Folly, is parting from
thee. The oracles still talked in their sleep, shall our
grand-children say, till Master Merriman's kingdom
was broken up: now is every man his own fool, and
the world's sign is taken down.

(He sings)

Folly hath now turned out of door
Mankind and Fate, who were before
    Jove's harlequin and clown:
For goosegrass-harvest now is o'er;
The world's no stage, no tavern more,
    Its sign, the Fool, 's ta'en down.

*   *   *

Wolfram. The earth may open, and the sea o'erwhelm;
Many the ways, the little home is one;
Thither the courser leads, thither the helm,
And at one gate we meet when all is done.

*   *   *

Isbr. The idiot merriment of thoughtless men!
How the fish laugh at them, that swim and toy
About the ruined ship, wrecked deep below,
Whose pilot's skeleton, all full of sea weeds,
Leans on his anchor, grinning like their Hope.

*   *   *

Aɛt II

SCENE I

DUKE MELVERIC of Munsterberg, rescued by WOLFRAM, ISBRAND'S brother, from the Saracens in Egypt, has there killed him out of jealousy for SIBYLLA and now returns, disguised, with the corpse.

The interior of a church at Ancona. The DUKE, *in the garb of a pilgrim,* SIBYLLA *and Knights, assembled round the corpse of* WOLFRAM, *which is lying on a bier.*

DIRGE

If thou wilt ease thine heart
Of love and all its smart,
    Then sleep, dear, sleep;
And not a sorrow
  Hang any tear on your eyelashes;
    Lie still and deep,
  Sad soul, until the sea-wave washes
The rim o' the sun to-morrow,
    In eastern sky.

But wilt thou cure thine heart
Of love and all its smart,
    Then die, dear, die;
'Tis deeper, sweeter,
  Than on a rose bank to lie dreaming
    With folded eye;
  And then alone, amid the beaming
Of love's stars, thou'lt meet her
    In eastern sky.

Knight. These rites completed, say your further pleasure.

Duke. To horse and homewards in all haste: my
    business
Urges each hour. This body bury here,
With all due honours. I myself will build
A monument, whereon, in after times,
Those of his blood shall read his valiant deeds,
And see the image of the bodily nature
He was a man in. Scarcely dare I, lady,
Mock you with any word of consolation:
But soothing care, and silence o'er that sorrow,
Which thine own tears alone may tell to thee
Or offer comfort for; and in all matters
What thy will best desires, I promise thee.
Wilt thou hence with us?
    Sibyl.   Whither you will lead me.
My will lies there, my hope, and all my life
Which was in this world. Yet if I shed a tear,
It is not for his death, but for my life.
Dead is he? Say not so, but that he is
No more excepted from Eternity.
If he were dead I should indeed despair.
Can Wolfram die? Ay, as the sun doth set:
It is the earth that falls away from light;
Fixed in the heavens, although unseen by us,
The immortal life and light remains triumphant.
And therefore you shall never see me wail,
Or drop base waters of an ebbing sorrow;
No wringing hands, no sighings, no despair,
No mourning weeds will I betake me to;
But keep my thought of him that is no more,
As secret as great nature keeps his soul,
From all the world; and consecrate my being

To that divinest hope, which none can know of
Who have not laid their dearest in the grave.
Farewell, my love,—I will not say to thee,
"Pale corpse",—we do not part for many days.
A little sleep, a little waking more,
And then we are together out of life.
    Duke. Cover the coffin up. This cold, calm stare
Upon familiar features is most dreadful:
Methinks too the expression of the face
Is changed, since all was settled gently there;
And threatens now. But I have sworn to speak
And think of that no more, which has been done—
Now then into the bustle of the world!
We'll rub our cares smooth there.

*   *   *

Act II

SCENE II
*   *

    Athulf.   What need of asking?
You know the man is sore upon a couch;
But upright, on his bloody-hoofèd steed
Galloping o'er the ruins of his foes,
Whose earthquake he hath been, then will he shout,
Laugh, run his tongue along his trembling lip,
And swear his heart tastes honey.
    Siegfried.   Nay, thou'rt harsh;
He was the axe of Mars; but, Troy being felled,
Peace trims her bower with him.
    Athulf.   Ay; in her hand
He's iron still.

*   *   *

In the castle of Munsterberg at Grüssau in Silesia the DUKE'S two sons,
the warlike ADALMAR and the soft ATHULF, discuss their love for AMALA.

*   *   *

Adalm.   Joyous creature!
Whose life's first leaf is hardly yet uncurled.
    Athulf. Use your trade's language; were I journey-
man
To Mars, the glorious butcher, I would say
She's sleek, and sacrificial flowers would look well
On her white front.
    Adalm.   Now, brother, can you think,
Stern as I am above, that in my depth
There is no cleft wherein such thoughts are hived
As from dear looks and words come back to me,
Storing that honey, love? O! love I do,
Through every atom of my being.
    Athulf.   Ay,
So do we young ones all. In winter time
This god of butterflies, this Cupid sleeps,
As they do in their cases; but May comes;
With it the bee and he: each spring of mine
He sends me a new arrow, thank the boy.
A week ago he shot me for this year;
The shaft is in my stomach, and so large
There's scarcely room for dinner.
    Adalm.   Shall I believe thee,
Or judge mortality by this stout sample
I screw my mail o'er? Well, it may be so;
You are an adept in these chamber passions,
And have a heart that's Cupid's arrow-cushion,
Worn out with use. I never knew before

The meaning of this love. But one has taught me,
It is a heaven wandering among men,
The spirit of gone Eden haunting earth.
Life's joys, death's pangs are viewless from its bosom,
Which they who keep are gods; there's no paradise,
There is no heaven, no angels, no blessed spirits
No souls, or they have no eternity,
If this be not a part of them.
   Athulf.   This in a Court!
Such sort of love might Hercules have felt
Warm from the Hydra fight, when he had fattened
On a fresh-slain Bucentaur, roasted whole,
The heart of his pot-belly, till it ticked
Like a cathedral clock. But in good faith
Is this the very truth? Then have I found
My fellow fool. For I am wounded too
E'en to the quick and inmost, Adalmar.
So fair a creature! of such charms compact
As nature stints elsewhere; which you may find
Under the tender eyelid of a serpent,
Or in the gurge of a kiss-coloured rose,
By drops and sparks: but when she moves, you see,
Like water from a crystal overfilled,
Fresh beauty tremble out of her and lave
Her fair sides to the ground. Of other women,
(And we have beauteous in this court of ours,)
I can remember whether nature touched
Their eye with brown or azure, where a vein
Runs o'er a sleeping eyelid, like some streak
In a young blossom; every grace count up,
Here the round turn and crevice of the arm,

There the tress-bunches, or the slender hand
Seen between harpstrings gathering music from them:
But where she is, I'm lost in her abundance
And when she leaves me I know nothing more,
(Like one from whose awakening temples rolls
The cloudy vision of a god away,)
Than that she was divine.

*   *   *

Act II

SCENE III. *A retired gallery in the ducal castle*

ISBRAND plots with his accomplice SIEGFRIED to overthrow the
DUKE'S deputy, THORWALD, in vengeance for WOLFRAM.

Enter ISBRAND *and* SIEGFRIED

Isbr. Now see you how this dragon egg of ours
Swells with its ripening plot? Methinks I hear
Snaky rebellion turning restless in it,
And with its horny jaws scraping away
The shell that hides it. All is ready now:
I hold the latch-string of a new world's wicket;
One pull and it rolls in. Bid all our friends
Meet in that ruinous church-yard once again,
By moonrise: until then I'll hide myself;
For these sweet thoughts rise dimpling to my lips,
And break the dark stagnation of my features,
Like sugar melting in a glass of poison.
To-morrow, Siegfried, shalt thou see me sitting
One of the drivers of this racing earth,
With Grüssau's reins between my fingers. Ha!
Never since Hell laughed at the church, blood-drunken
From rack and wheel, has there been joy so mad
As that which stings my marrow now.

Siegfr.   Good cause,
The sun-glance of a coming crown to heat you,
And give your thoughts gay colours in the steam
Of a fermenting brain.
  Isbr.   Not alone that.
A sceptre is smooth handling, it is true,
And one grows fat and jolly in a chair
That has a kingdom crouching under it,
With one's name on its collar, like a dog,
To fetch and carry. But the heart I have
Is a strange little snake. He drinks not wine,
When he'd be drunk, but poison: he doth fatten
On bitter hate, not love. And, O that duke!
My life is hate of him; and, when I tread
His neck into the grave, I shall, methinks,
Fall into ashes with the mighty joy,
Or be transformed into a wingèd star:
That will be all eternal heaven distilled
Down to one thick rich minute. This sounds madly,
But I am mad when I remember him:
Siegfried, you know not why.
  Siegfr.   I never knew
That you had quarrelled.
  Isbr.   True: but did you see
My brother's corpse? There was a wound on't, Siegfried;
He died not gently, nor in a ripe age;
And I'll be sworn it was the duke that did it,
Else he had not remained in that far land,
And sent his knights to us again.
  Siegfr.   I thought
He was the duke's close friend.

Isbr.   Close as his blood:
A double-bodied soul they did appear,
Rather than fellow hearts.
   Siegfr.   I've heard it told
That they did swear and write in their best blood,
And her's they loved the most, that who died first
Should, on death's holidays, revisit him
Who still dwelt in the flesh.
   Isbr.   O that such bond
Would move the jailor of the grave to open
Life's gate again unto my buried brother,
But half an hour! Were I buried, like him,
There in the very garrets of death's town,
But six feet under earth, (that's the grave's sky,)
I'd jump up into life. But he's a quiet ghost;
He walks not in the churchyard after dew,
But gets to his grave betimes, burning no glow-worms,
Sees that his bones are right, and stints his worms
Most miserly. If you were murdered, Siegfried,
As he was by this duke, should it be so?
   Siegfr. Here speaks again your passion: what know we
Of Death's commandments to his subject-spirits,
Who are as yet the body's citizens?
What seas unnavigable, what wild forests,
What castles, and what ramparts there may hedge
His icy frontier?
   Isbr.   Tower and roll what may,
There have been goblins bold who have stolen passports
Or sailed the sea, or leaped the wall, or flung
The drawbridge down, and travelled back again.
So would my soul have done. But let it be.

At the doom-twilight shall the ducal cut-throat
Wake by a tomb-fellow he little dreamt of.
Methinks I see them rising with mixed bones,
A pair of patch-work angels.
    Siegfr.   What does this mean?
   Isbr. A pretty piece of kidnapping, that's all.
When Melveric's heart's heart, his new-wed wife,
Upon the bed whereon she bore these sons,
Died, as a blossom does whose inmost fruit
Tears it in twain, and in its stead remains
A bitter poison-berry: when she died,
What her soul left was by her husband laid
In the marriage grave, whereto he doth consign
Himself when dead.
    Siegfr.   Like a true loving mate.
Is not her tomb 'mid the cathedral ruins,
Where we to-night assemble?
    Isbr.   Say not her's:
A changeling lies there. By black night came I,
And, while a man might change two goblets' liquors,
I laid the lips of their two graves together.
And poured my brother into hers; while she,
Being the lightest, floated and ran over.
Now lies the murdered where the loved should be;
And Melveric the dead shall dream of heaven,
Embracing his damnation. There's revenge.
But hush! here comes one of my dogs, the princes;
To work with you!   [*Exit* SIEGFRIED

      *   *   *

Aᑔ III

SCENE III

ISBRAND gathers in the churchyard his conspirators, including the
DUKE'S own son, ADALMAR, and the DUKE himself, still disguised as a
pilgrim.

*   *   *

Adalm.   Enough. How are the citizens?
You feasted them these three days.
    Isbr.   And have them by the heart for't.
'Neath Grüssau's tiles sleep none, whose deepest bosom
My fathom hath not measured; none, whose thoughts
I have not made a map of. In the depth
And labyrinthine home of the still soul,
Where the seen thing is imaged, and the whisper
Joints the expecting spirit, my spies, which are
Suspicion's creeping words, have stolen in,
And, with their eyed feelers, touched and sounded
The little hiding holes of cunning thought,
And each dark crack in which a reptile purpose
Hangs in its chrysalis unripe for birth.
All of each heart I know.
    Duke.   O perilous boast!
Fathom the wavy caverns of all stars,
Know every side of every sand in earth,
And hold in little all the lore of man,
As a dew's drop doth miniature the sun:
But never hope to learn the alphabet,
In which the hieroglyphic human soul
More changeably is painted, than the rainbow

Upon the cloudy pages of a shower,
Whose thunderous hinges a wild wind doth turn.
Know all of each! when each doth shift his thought
More often in a minute, than the air
Dust on a summer path.
    Isbr.   Liquors can lay them:
Grape-juice or vein-juice.

*   *   *

Exeunt: manet DUKE

    Duke. I'm old and desolate. O were I dead
With thee, my wife! Oft have I lain by night
Upon thy grave, and burned with the mad wish
To raise thee up to life. Thank God, whom then
I might have thought not pitiful, for lending
No ear to such a prayer. Far better were I
Thy grave-fellow, than thou alive with me,
Amid the fears and perils of the time.

Enter ZIBA

Who's in the dark there?
    Ziba.   One of the dark's colour:
Ziba, thy slave.
    Duke.   Come at a wish, my Arab.
Is Thorwald's house asleep yet?
    Ziba.   No: his lights still burn.
    Duke. Go; fetch a lantern and some working fellows
With spade and pickaxe. Let not Thorwald come.
In good speed do it.   [*Exit* ZIBA
              That alone is left me:
I will abandon this ungrateful country,

And leave my dukedom's earth behind me; all,
Save the small urn that holds my dead beloved:
That relic will I save from my wrecked princedom;
Beside it live and die.

(Enter THORWALD, ZIBA, and gravediggers)

        Thorwald with them!
Old friend, I hoped you were in pleasant sleep:
'Tis a late walking hour.
  Thorw.   I came to learn
Whether the slave spoke true. This haunted hour,
What would you with the earth? Dig you for treasure?
  Duke. Ay, I do dig for treasure. To the vault,
Lift up the kneeling marble woman there,
And delve down to the coffin. Ay, for treasure:
The very dross of such a soul and body
Shall stay no longer in this land of hate.
I'll covetously rake the ashes up
Of this my love-consumed incense-star,
And in a golden urn, over whose sides
An unborn life of sculpture shall be poured,
They shall stand ever on my chamber altar.
I am not Heaven's rebel; think't not of me;
Nor that I'd trouble her sepulchral sleep
For a light end. Religiously I come
To change the bed of my beloved lady,
That what remains below of us may join,
Like its immortal.
  Thorw.   There is no ill here:
And yet this breaking through the walls, that sever
The quick and cold, led never yet to good.

Ziba. Our work is done: betwixt the charmed moon-
    shine
And the coffin lies nought but a nettle's shade,
That shakes its head at the deed.
    Duke.   Let the men go.   [*Exeunt labourers*
                    Now Death, thou shadowy miser,
I am thy robber; be not merciful,
But take me in requital. There is she then;
I cannot hold my tears, thinking how altered.
O thoughts, ye fleeting, unsubstantial family!
Thou formless, viewless, and unuttered memory!
How dare ye yet survive that gracious image,
Sculptured about the essence whence ye rose?
That words of hers should ever dwell in me,
Who is as if she never had been born
To all earth's millions, save this one! Nay, prithee,
Let no one comfort me. I'll mourn awhile
Over her memory.
    Thorw.   Let the past be past,
And Lethe freeze unwept-on over it.
What is, be patient with: and, with what shall be,
Silence the body-bursting spirit's yearnings.
Thou say'st that, when she died, that day was spilt
All beauty flesh could hold; that day went down
An oversouled creation. The time comes
When thou shalt find again thy blessed love,
Pure from all earth, and with the usury
Of her heaven-hoarded charms.
    Duke.   Is this the silence
That I commanded? Fool, thou say'st a lesson
Out of some philosophic pedant's book.

I loved no desolate soul: she was a woman,
Whose spirit I knew only through those limbs,
Those tender members thou dost dare despise;
By whose exhaustless beauty, infinite love,
Trackless expression only, I did learn
That there was aught yet viewless and eternal;
Since they could come from such alone. Where is she?
Where shall I ever see her as she was?
With the sweet smile, she smiled only on me;
With those eyes full of thoughts, none else could see?
Where shall I meet that brow and lip with mine?
Hence with thy shadows! But her warm fair body,
Where's that? There, mouldered to the dust. Old man,
If thou dost dare to mock my ears again
With thy ridiculous, ghostly consolation,
I'll send thee to the blessings thou dost speak of.
    Thorw. For Heaven's and her sake restrain this
      passion.
    Duke. She died. But Death is old and half worn out:
Are there no chinks in't? Could she not come to me?
Ghosts have been seen; but never in a dream,
After she'd sighed her last, was she the blessing
Of these desiring eyes. All, save my soul,
And that but for her sake, were his who knew
The spell of Endor, and could raise her up.
    Thorw. Another time that thought were impious.
Unreasonable longings, such as these,
Fit not your age and reason. In sorrow's rage
Thou dost demand and bargain for a dream,
Which children smile at in their tales.
    Ziba.   Smile ignorance!

But, sure as men have died, strong necromancy
Hath set the clock of time and nature back;
And made Earth's rooty, ruinous, grave-floored caverns
Throb with the pangs of birth. Ay, were I ever
Where the accused innocent did pray
Acquittal from dead lips, I would essay
My sires' sepulchral magic.

Duke.   Slave, thou tempt'st me
To lay my sword's point to thy throat, and say
"Do it or die thyself".

Thorw.   Prithee, come in.
To cherish hopes like these is either madness,
Or a sure cause of it. Come in and sleep:
To-morrow we'll talk further.

Duke.   Go in thou.
Sleep blinds no eyes of mine, till I have proved
This slave's temptation.

Thorw.   Then I leave you to him.
Good-night again.   [*Exit* THORWALD

Duke.   Good-night, and quiet slumbers.
Now then, thou juggling African, thou shadow,
Think'st thou I will not murder thee this night,
If thou again dare tantalize my soul
With thy accursed hints, thy lying boasts?
Say, shall I stab thee?

Ziba.   Then thou murder'st truth.
I spoke of what I'd do.

Duke.   You told ghost-lies,
And held me for a fool because I wept.
Now, once more, silence: or to-night I shed
Drops royaller and redder than those tears.

Enter ISBRAND *and* SIEGFRIED

Isbr. Pilgrim, not yet abed? Why, ere you've time
To lay your cloak down, heaven will strip off night,
And show her daily bosom.
    Duke.   Sir, my eyes
Never did feel less appetite for sleep:
I and my slave intend to watch till morrow.
    Isbr. Excellent. You're a fellow of my humour.
I never sleep o' nights: the black sky likes me,
And the soul's solitude, while half mankind
Lie quiet in earth's shade and rehearse death.
Come, let's be merry: I have sent for wine,
And here it comes.   [*It is brought in*
                    These mossy stones about us
Will serve for stools, although they have been turrets
Which scarce aught touched but sunlight, or the claw
Of the strong-wingèd eagles, who lived here
And fed on battle-bones. Come sit, sir stranger;
Sit too, my devil-coloured one; here's room
Upon my rock. Fill, Siegfried.
    Siegfr.   Yellow wine,
And rich, be sure. How like you it?
    Duke.   Better ne'er wetted lip.
    Isbr. Then fill again. Come, hast no song to-night,
Siegfried? Nor you, my midnight of a man?
I'm weary of dumb toping.
    Siegfr.   Yet you sing not.
My songs are staler than the cuckoo's tune:
And you, companions?
    Duke.   We are quite unused.
    Isbr. Then you shall have a ballad of my making.

Siegfr.   How? do you rhyme too?
Isbr. Sometimes, in rainy weather.
Here's what I made one night, while picking poisons
To make the rats a salad.
Duke.   And what's your tune?
Isbr. What is the night-bird's tune, wherewith she
     startles
The bee out of his dream, that turns and kisses
The inmost of his flower and sleeps again?
What is the lobster's tune when he is boiling?
I hate your ballads that are made to come
Round like a squirrel's cage, and round again.
We nightingales sing boldly from our hearts:
So listen to us

            *   *   *

Isbr. Methinks that earth and heaven are grown bad
     neighbours,
And have blocked up the common door between
     them.
Five hundred years ago had we sat here
So late and lonely, many a jolly ghost
Would have joined company.
Siegfr.   To trust in story,
In the old times Death was a feverish sleep,
In which men walked. The other world was cold
And thinly-peopled, so life's emigrants
Came back to mingle with the crowds of earth:
But now great cities are transplanted thither,
Memphis, and Babylon, and either Thebes,
And Priam's towery town with its one beech,

And dead are most and merriest: so be sure
There will be no more haunting, till their towns
Are full to the garret; then they'll shut their gates,
To keep the living out, and perhaps leave
A dead or two between both kingdoms.

        *   *   *

   Duke. Obstinate slave! Now that we are alone,
Durst thou again say life and soul has lifted
The dead man from the grave, and sent him walking
Over the earth?
   Ziba.   I say it, and will add
Deed to my word, not oath. Within that tomb
Dwells he, whom you would call?
   Duke.   There. But stand off!
If you do juggle with her holy bones,
By God I'll murder thee. I don't believe you,
For here next to my heart I wear a bond,
Written in the blood of one who was my friend,
In which he swears that, dying first, he would
Borrow some night his body from the ground,
To visit me once more. One day we quarrelled,
Swords hung beside us and we drew: he fell.
Yet never has his bond or his revenge
Raised him to my bed-side, haunting his murderer,
Or keeping blood-sealed promise to his friend.
Does not this prove you lie?
   Ziba.   'Tis not my spell:
Shall I try that with him?
   Duke.   No, no! not him.
The heavy world press on him, where he lies,
With all her towers and mountains!

Ziba.   Listen, Lord.
Time was when Death was young and pitiful,
Though callous now by use: and then there dwelt,
In the thin world above, a beauteous Arab,
Unmated yet and boyish. To his couch
At night, which shone so starry through the boughs,
A pale flower-breathed nymph with dewy hair
Would often come, but all her love was silent;
And ne'er by day-light could he gaze upon her,
For ray by ray, as morning came, she paled,
And like a snow of air dissolv'd i' th' light,
Leaving behind a stalk with lilies hung,
Round which her womanish graces had assembled.
So did the early love-time of his youth
Pass with delight: but when, compelled at length,
He left the wilds and woods for riotous camps
And cities full of men, he saw no more,
Tho' prayed and wept for, his old bed-time vision,
The pale dissolving maiden. He would wander
Sleepless about the waste, benighted fields,
Asking the speechless shadows of his thoughts
"Who shared my couch? Who was my love? Where
     is she?"
Thus passing through a grassy burial-ground,
Wherein a new-dug grave gaped wide for food,
"Who was she?" cried he, and the earthy mouth
Did move its nettle-bearded lips together,
And said "'Twas I—I, Death: behold our child!"
The wanderer looked, and on the lap of the pit
A young child slept as at a mother's breast.
He raised it and he reared it. From that infant

My race, the death-begotten, draw their blood:
Our prayer for the diseased works more than
    medicine;
Our blessings oft secure grey hairs and happy
To new-born infants; and, in case of need,
The dead and gone are re-begotten by us,
And motherlessly born to second life.
    Duke. I've heard your tale. Now exorcise: but
    mark!
If thou dost dare to make my heart thy fool,
I'll send thee to thy grave-mouthed grandam, Arab.
    Ziba. Wilt thou submit unmurmuring to all evils,
Which this recall to a forgotten being
May cause to thee and thine?
    Duke.   With all my soul,
So I may take the good.
    Ziba.   And art thou ready
To follow, if so be its will, the ghost,
Whom you will re-imbody, to the place
Which it doth now inhabit?
    Duke.   My first wish.
Now to your sorcery: and no more conditions,
In hopes I may break off. All ill be mine,
Which shall the world revisit with the being
That lies within.
    Ziba.   Enough. Upon this scroll
Are written words, which read, even in a whisper,
Would in the air create another star;
And, more than thunder-tongued storms in the sky,
Make the old world to quake and sweat with fear;
And, as the chilly damps of her death-swoon

Fall and condense, they to the moon reflect
The forms and colours of the pale old dead.
Laid there among the bones, and left to burn
With sacred spices, its keen vaporous power
Would draw to life the earliest dead of all,
Swift as the sun doth ravish a dew-drop
Out of a flower. But see, the torch-flame dies:
How shall I light it?

    Duke.   Here's my useless blood-bond;
These words, that should have waked illumination
Within a corpse's eyes, will make a tinder,
Whose sparks might be of life instead of fire.
Burn it.

    Ziba. An incense for thy senses, god of those,
To whom life is as death to us; who were,
Ere our grey ancestors wrote history;
When these our ruined towers were in the rock;
And our great forests, which do feed the sea
With storm-souled fleets, lay in an acorn's cup:
When all was seed that now is dust; our minute
Invisibly far future. Send thy spirit
From plant of the air, and from the air and earth,
And from earth's worms, and roots, again to gather
The dispersed being, 'mid whose bones I place
The words which, spoken, shall destroy death's
    kingdom,
And which no voice, but thunder, can pronounce.
Marrow fill bone, and vine-like veins run round
    them,
And flesh, thou grass, mown wert thou long ago,—
Now comes the brown dry after-crop. Ho! ghost!

There's thy old heart a-beating, and thy life
Burning on the old hearth.. Come home again!
    Duke. Hush! Do you hear a noise?
    Ziba.   It is the sound
Of the ghost's foot on Jacob's ladder-rungs.
    Duke. More like the tread upon damp stony steps
Out of a dungeon. Dost thou hear a door
Drop its great bolt and grate upon its hinges?
    Ziba. Serpentine Hell! That is thy staircase
      echo,   [*aside*
And thy jaws' groaning. What betides it?
    Duke. Thou human murder-time of night,
What hast thou done?
    Ziba. My task: give me to death, if the air has not
What was the earth's but now. Ho there! i' th' vault.
    A Voice. Who breaks my death?
    Ziba. Draw on thy body, take up thy old limbs,
And then come forth tomb-born.
    Duke.   One moment's peace!
Let me remember what a grace she had,
Even in her dying hour: her soul set not,
But at its noon Death like a cloud came o'er it,
And now hath passed away. O come to me,
Thou dear returned spirit of my wife;
And, surely as I clasp thee once again,
Thou shalt not die without me.
    Ziba.   Ho! there, Grave,
Is life within thee?
    The Voice.   Melveric, I am here.
    Duke. Did'st hear that whisper? Open, and let in
The blessing to my eyes, whose subtle breath

Doth penetrate my heart's quick; and let me hear
That dearest name out of those dearest lips.
Who comes back to my heart?

(MANDRAKE *runs out of the sepulchre*)

Ziba.   Momus of Hell, what's this?
Duke. Is this thy wretched jest, thou villanous fool?
But I will punish thee, by heaven; and thou too
                                        [*To* MANDRAKE
Shalt soon be what thou should'st have better acted.

Mandr. Excuse me: as you have thought proper to
call me to the living, I shall take the liberty of remaining
alive. If you want to speak to another ghost, of longer
standing, look into the old lumber-room of a vault
again: some one seems to be putting himself together
there. Good-night, gentlemen, for I must travel to
Egypt once more.   [*Exit*

Duke. Thou disappointed cheat! Was this a fellow,
Whom thou hadst hired to act a spectral part?
Thou see'st how well he does it. But away!
Or I will teach thee better to rehearse it.

Ziba. Death is a hypocrite then, a white dissembler,
Like all that doth seem good! I am put to shame.
                                                [*Exit*

Duke. Deceived and disappointed vain desires!
Why laugh I not, and ridicule myself?
'Tis still, and cold, and nothing in the air
But an old grey twilight, or of eve or morn,
I know not which, dim as futurity,
And sad and hoary as the ghostly past,
Fills up the space. Hush! not a wind is there,
Not a cloud sails over the battlements,

Not a bell tolls the hour. Is there an hour?
Or is not all gone by, which here did hive,
Of men and their life's ways? Could I but hear
The ticking of a clock, or some one breathing,
Or e'en a cricket's chirping, or the grating
Of the old gates amidst the marble tombs,
I should be sure that this was still the world.
Hark! Hark! Doth nothing stir?
No light, and still no light, besides this ghost
That mocks the dawn, unaltered? Still no sound?
No voice of man? No cry of beast? No rustle
Of any moving creature? And sure I feel
That I remain the same: no more round blood-drops
Roll joyously along my pulseless veins:
The air I seem to breathe is still the same:
And the great dreadful thought, that now comes o'er me,
Must remain ever as it is, unchanged—
This moment doth endure for evermore;
Eternity hath overshadowed time;
And I alone am left of all that lived,
Pent in this narrow, horrible conviction.
Ha! the dead soon will wake! My Agnes, rise;
Rise up, my wife! One look, ere Wolfram comes;
Quick, or it is too late: the murdered hasten:
My best-beloved, come once to my heart...
But ah! who art thou?

(*The gates of the sepulchre fly open and discover* WOLFRAM)

Wolfr.   Wolfram, murderer,
To whose heart thou didst come with horrid purpose.
  Duke. Lie of my eyes, begone! Art thou not dead?

Are not the worms, that ate thy marrow, dead?
What dost thou here, thou wretched goblin fool?
Think'st thou, I fear thee? Thou man-mocking air,
Thou art not truer than a mirror's image,
Nor half so lasting. Back again to coffin,
Thou baffled idiot spectre, or haunt cradles;
Or stay, and I'll laugh at thee. Guard thyself,
If thou pretendest life.
 Wolfr. Is this thin air, that thrusts thy sword away?
Flesh, bones, and soul, and blood that thou stol'st
  from me.
Upon thy summons, bound by heart-red letters,
Here Wolfram stands: what wouldst thou?
 Duke.   What sorcery else,
But that cursed compact, could have made full Hell
Boil over, and spill thee, thou topmost damned?
But down again! I'll see no more of thee.
Hound, to thy kennel, to your coffin, bones,
Ghost, to thy torture!
 Wolfr.   Thou returnest with me;
So make no hurry. I will stay awhile
To see how the old world goes, feast and be merry,
And then to work again.
 Duke.   Darest thou stand there,
Thou shameless vapour, and assert thyself,
While I defy, and question, and deride thee?
The stars, I see them dying: clearly all
The passage of this night remembrance gives me,
And I think coolly: but my brain is mad,
Else why behold I that? Is't possible
Thou'rt true, and worms have vomited thee up

Upon this rind of earth? No; thou shalt vanish.
Was it for this I hated thee and killed thee?
I'll have thee dead again, and hounds and eagles
Shall be thy graves, since this old, earthy one
Hath spat thee out for poison.
  Wolfr.   Thou, old man,
Art helpless against me. I shall not harm thee;
So lead me home. I am not used to sunlight,
And morn's a-breaking.
  Duke.   Then there is rebellion
Against all kings, even Death. Murder's worn out
And full of holes; I'll never make't the prison,
Of what I hate, again. Come with me, spectre;
If thou wilt live against the body's laws,
Thou murderer of Nature, it shall be
A question, which haunts which, while thou dost last.
So come with me.
               [Exeunt

Act IV

SCENE III

AMALA is being prepared for her wedding with ADALMAR

*   *   *

 Bridesmaid. Take this flower from me
(A white rose, fitting for a wedding-gift,)
And lay it on your pillow. Pray to live
So fair and innocently; pray to die,
Leaf after leaf, so softly.

*   *   *

Enter singers and musicians led by SIEGFRIED; *they play under*
the windows of AMALA'S *apartment, and sing*

SONG
By female voices
We have bathed, where none have seen us,
    In the lake and in the fountain,
        Underneath the charmèd statue
Of the timid, bending Venus,
    When the water-nymphs were counting
In the waves the stars of night,
        And those maidens started at you,
Your limbs shone through so soft and bright.
        But no secrets dare we tell,
            For thy slaves unlace thee,
            And he, who shall embrace thee,
        Waits to try thy beauty's spell.

By male voices
We have crowned thee queen of women,
    Since love's love, the rose, hath kept her
        Court within thy lips and blushes,
And thine eye, in beauty swimming,
    Kissing, we rendered up the sceptre,
At whose touch the startled soul
        Like an ocean bounds and gushes,
And spirits bend at thy controul.
        But no secrets dare we tell,
            For thy slaves unlace thee,
            And he, who shall embrace thee,
        Is at hand, and so farewell.

*   *   *

SONG by *Siegfried*

Lady, was it fair of thee
To seem so passing fair to me?
  Not every star to every eye
    Is fair: and why
Art thou another's share?
  Did thine eyes shed brighter glances,
Thine unkissed bosom heave more fair,
  To his than to my fancies?
    But I'll forgive thee still;
    Thou'rt fair without thy will.
    So be: but never know,
    That 'tis the hue of woe.

Lady, was it fair of thee
To be so gentle still to me?
  Not every lip to every eye
    Should let smiles fly.
Why didst thou never frown,
  To frighten from my pillow
Love's head, round which Hope wove a crown,
  And saw not 'twas of willow?
    But I'll forgive thee still;
    Thou knew'st not smiles could kill.
    Smile on: but never know,
    I die, nor of what woe.

*   *   *

ATHULF has swallowed poison procured from ZIBA, in jealousy of his
brother ADALMAR'S marriage to AMALA; then, with a revulsion, has
begged ADALMAR to go and get from ZIBA an antidote. Meanwhile
AMALA has confessed to the dying ATHULF that it is he that she really
loves, not his brother.

Exit AMALA

Athulf. Farewell, my bliss! She loves me with her
 soul,
And I might have enjoyed her, were he fallen.
Ha! ha! and I am dying like a rat,
And he shall drink his wine, twenty years hence,
Beside his cherished wife, and speak of me
With a compassionate smile! Come, Madness, come,
For death is loitering still.

Enter ADALMAR *and* ZIBA

Adalm.   An antidote!
Restore him whom thy poisons have laid low,
If thou wilt not sup with thy fellow fiends
In hell to-night.
Ziba.   I pray thee strike me not.
It was his choice; and why should he be breathing
Against his will?
Athulf.   Ziba, I need not perish.
Now my intents are changed: so, if thou canst,
Dispense me life again.
Adalm.   Listen to him, slave,
And once be a preserver.
Ziba.   Let him rise.
Why, think you that I'd deal a benefit,
So precious to the noble as is death,

To such a pampered darling of delight
As he that shivers there? O, not for him,
Blooms my dark Nightshade, nor doth Hemlock brew
Murder for cups within her cavernous root.
Not for him is the metal blessed to kill,
Nor lets the poppy her leaves fall for him.
To heroes such are sacred. He may live,
As long as 'tis the Gout and Dropsy's pleasure.
He wished to play at suicide, and swallowed
A draught, that may depress and shake his powers
Until he sleeps awhile; then all is o'er.
And so good-night, my princes.   [*Exit*

*   *   *

Act IV

SCENE IV

ISBRAND hears that his plot has succeeded and he is master of Grüssau.

*   *   *

  Isbr. O! it is nothing now to be a man.
Adam, thy soul was happy when it wore
The first new, mortal members. To have felt
The joy of the first year, when the one spirit
Kept house-warming within its fresh-built clay,
I'd be content to be as old a ghost.
Thine was the hour to live in. Now we're common,
And man is tired of being merely human;
And I'll be something more; yet, not by tearing
This chrysalis of psyche ere its hour,
Will I break through Elysium. There are sometimes,

Even here, the means of being more than men:
And I by wine, and women, and the sceptre,
Will be, my own way, heavenly in my clay.
O you small star-mob, had I been one of you,
I would have seized the sky some moonless night,
And made myself the sun; whose morrow rising
Shall see me new-created by myself.
Come, come; to rest, my soul. I must sleep off
This old plebeian creature that I am.   [*Exit*

Aĉt V

SCENE II

SIEGFRIED plots against the successful ISBRAND

*   *   *

Ziba. Siegfried, I'll free you from this thankless
    master.
Siegfr. I understand. To-night? Why, that is best.
Man's greatest secret, like the earth's, the devil,
Slips through a keyhole or the smallest chink.
In plottings there is still some crack unstopped,
Some heart not air-tight, some fellow who doth talk
In sleep or in his cups, or tells his tale,
Love-drunk, unto his secret-selling mistress.
How shall't be done though?
    Ziba.   I'm his cup-bearer;
An office that he gave me in derision,
And I will execute so cunningly
That he shall have no lips, to laugh with, long;
Nor spare and spurn me, as he did last night.
Let him beware, who shows a dogged slave

Pity or mercy! For the drug, 'tis good:
There is a little, hairy, green-eyed snake,
Of voice like to the woody nightingale,
And ever singing pitifully sweet,
That nestles in the barry[1] bones of death,
And is his dearest pet and play-fellow.
The honied froth about that serpent's tongue
Deserves not so his habitation's name,
As doth the cup that I shall serve to him.   [*Exeunt*

Act V

SCENE III. *A meadow*

SIBYLLA *and ladies, gathering flowers*

Sibyl. Enough; the dew falls, and the glow-worm's
    shining:
Now let us search our basket for the fairest
Among our flowery booty, and then sort them.
    Lady. The snowdrops are all gone; but here are
    cowslips,
And primroses, upon whose petals maidens,
Who love to find a moral in all things,
May read a lesson of pale bashfulness;
And violets, that have taught their young buds whiteness,
That blue-eyed ladies' lovers might not tear them
For the old comparison; daisies without number,
And buttercups and lilies of the vale.
    Sibyl. Sit then; and we will bind some up with rushes,
And wind us garlands. Thus it is with man;
He looks on nature as his supplement,

---

[1] ? barren. Though "barry" may well be right.

And still will find out likenesses and tokens
Of consanguinity, in the world's graces,
To his own being. So he loves the rose,
For the cheek's sake, whose touch is the most grateful
At night-fall to his lip; and, as the stars rise,
Welcomes the memories of delighting glances,
Which go up as an answer o'er his soul.
    Lady. And therefore earth and all its ornaments,
Which are the symbols of humanity
In forms refined, and efforts uncompleted,
Graceful and innocent, temper the heart
Of him who muses and compares them skilfully,
To glad belief and tearful gratitude.
This is the sacred source of poesy.
    Sibyl. While we are young and free from care, we
      think so.
But, when old age or sorrow brings us nearer
To spirits and their interests, we see
Few features of mankind in outward nature;
But rather signs inviting us to heaven.
I love flowers too; not for a young girl's reason,
But because these brief visitors to us
Rise yearly from the neighbourhood of the dead,
To show us how far fairer and more lovely
Their world is; and return thither again,
Like parting friends that beckon us to follow,
And lead the way silent and smilingly.
Fair is the season when they come to us,
Unfolding the delights of that existence
Which is below us: 'tis the time of spirits,
Who with the flowers, and like them, leave their graves:

But when the earth is sealed, and none dare come
Upwards to cheer us, and man's left alone,
We have cold, cutting winter. For no bridal,
Excepting with the grave, are flowers fit emblems.
    Lady. And why then do we pluck and wreathe them
      now?
    Sibyl. Because a bridal with the grave is near.
You will have need of them to strew a corpse.
Ay, maidens, I am dying; but lament not:
It is to me a wished-for change of being.
Yonder behold the evening star arising,
Appearing bright over the mountain-tops;
He has just died out of another region,
Perhaps a cloudy one; and so die I;
And the high heaven, serene and light with joy,
Which I pass into, will be my love's soul,
That will encompass me; and I shall tremble,
A brilliant star of never-dying delight,
'Mid the ethereal depth of his eternity.
Now lead me homewards: and I'll lay me down,
To sleep not, but to rest: then strew me o'er
With these flowers fresh from out of the ghosts' abodes,
And they will lead me softly down to them.   [*Exeunt*

Act V

SCENE IV

*   *   *

SONG

Old Adam, the carrion crow,
  The old crow of Cairo;
He sat in the shower, and let it flow
    Under his tail and over his crest;
      And through every feather
      Leaked the wet weather;
    And the bough swung under his nest;
    For his beak it was heavy with marrow.
      Is that the wind dying? O no;
      It's only two devils, that blow
      Through a murderer's bones, to and fro,
        In the ghosts' moonshine.

Ho! Eve, my grey carrion wife,
  When we have supped on kings' marrow,
Where shall we drink and make merry our life?
    Our nest it is queen Cleopatra's skull,
      'Tis cloven and cracked,
      And battered and hacked,
    But with tears of blue eyes it is full:
    Let us drink then, my raven of Cairo.
      Is that the wind dying? O no;
      It's only two devils, that blow
      Through a murderer's bones, to and fro,
        In the ghosts' moonshine.

*   *   *

L'ENVOI

*　　　　*　　　　*

Death's darts are sometimes Love's. So Nature tells,
When laughing waters close o'er drowning men;
When in flowers' honied corners poison dwells;
When Beauty dies: and the unwearied ken,
Of those who seek a cure for long despair,
Will learn. Death hath his dimples everywhere;
Love only on the cheek, which is to me most fair.

THE SECOND BROTHER

Aɛt I

SCENE I. *A street in Ferrara*

MICHELE *and* BATTISTA *meeting*: MARCELLO *at the side*

Michele. Fair shine this evening's stars upon your
    pleasures,
Battista Sorbi!
    Batt.   Sir, well met to-night:
Methinks our path is one.
    Michele.   And all Ferrara's.
There's not a candle lit to-night at home;
And for the cups,—they'll be less wet with wine
Than is the inmost grain of all this earth
With the now-falling dew. None sit indoors,
Except the babe, and his forgotten grandsire,
And such as, out of life, each side do lie
Against the shutter of the grave or womb.
The rest that build up the great hill of life,
From the crutch-riding boy to his sweet mother,
The deer-eyed girl, and the brown fellow of war,
To the grey-head and grandest sire of all
That's half in heaven,—all these are forth to-night;
And there they throng upon both sides the river,
Which, guessing at its hidden banks, flows on,
A water-stream betwixt two tides of flesh:—
And still the streets pour on, each drop a man;
You'd think the deluge was turned upside down,
And flesh was drowning water.

Batt.   Where go they?
To the feast, the wine, the lady-footed dance—
Where you, and I, and every citizen
That has a feathered and a jewelled cap,
And youthful curls to hang beside it brownly,—
To the Duke's brother, Lord Orazio's palace.
  Marc. (*aside*). Orazio! what of him?
  Michele.   Ay, that's a man
After the heart of Bacchus! By my life,
There is no mortal stuff, that foots the earth,
Able to wear the shape of man, like him,
And fill it with the carriage of a god.
We're but the tools and scaffolding of men,
The lines, the sketch, and he the very thing:
And, if we share the name of manhood with him,
Thus in the woods the tattered, wool-hung briar,
And the base, bowing poplar, the winds' slave,
Are trees,—and so's the great and kingly oak,
Within whose branches, like a soul, does dwell
The sun's bold eagle:—as the villain fox,
The weazel, and the sneaking cur are beasts,—
While he, whose wine is in a giant's heart,
The royal lion has no bigger name.
Let men be trees, why then he is the oak;
Let men be beasts, he is their lion-master;
Let them be stars, and then he is a sun,
A sun whose beams are gold, the night his noon,
His summer-field a marble hall of banquets,
With jasper, onyx, amber-leavèd cups
On golden straws for flowers, and, for the dew,
Wine of the richest grape. So let's not talk

And breathe away the time, whose sands are thawed
Into such purple tears, but drink it off.
 Batt. Why then, away! let's fit our velvet arms,
And on together.—
 Marc. (advancing). Nobles of Ferrara,
My gentle lords, have pity for a man,
Whom fortune and the roundness of the world
Have, from his feeble footing on its top,
Flung to deep poverty. When I was born,
They hid my helplessness in purple wraps,
And cradled me within a jewelled crown.
But now—O bitter now!—what name of woe,
Beyond the knowledge of the lips of hell,
Is fitted to my poor and withering soul,
And its old, wretched dwelling?
 Batt.   What is this?
Methinks that a prae-adamite skeleton,
Burst from the grave in a stolen cloak of flesh,
Ragged and threadbare, from a witch's back,
Who lived an hundred years, would scarcely seem
More miserably old.
 Michele.   A wandering beggar,
Come to Ferrara with the daily lie,
That bears him bread. Come on, and heed him not.
The stocks, old sir, grow in our streets.

Enter a GENTLEMAN

          How now?
What's your news, sir?
 Gent.   He's coming through this street,
Orazio, wrapt, like Bacchus, in the hide

Of a specked panther, with his dancing nymphs,
And torches bright and many, as his slaves
Had gathered up the fragments of the sun
That fell just now. Hark! here his music comes.

Enter ORAZIO, *between* ARMIDA *and* ROSAURA, *attended*

Orazio. Thrice to the moon, and thrice unto the sun,
And thrice unto the lesser stars of night,
From tower and hill, by trump and cannon's voice,
Have I proclaimed myself a deity's son:
Not Alexander's father, Ammon old,
But ivied Bacchus, do I call my sire.
Hymn it once more.

SONG

Strew not earth with empty stars,
    Strew it not with roses,
Nor feathers from the crest of Mars,
    Nor summer's idle posies.
'Tis not the primrose-sandalled moon,
    Nor cold and silent morn,
Nor he that climbs the dusty noon,
Nor mower war with scythe that drops,
Stuck with helmed and turbaned tops
    Of enemies new-shorn.
Ye cups, ye lyres, ye trumpets know,
Pour your music, let it flow,
'Tis Bacchus' son who walks below.

Orazio. Now break that kiss, and answer me, my Hebe;
Has our great sire a planet in the sky,—
One of these lights?

Rosau.   Not yet, I think, my lord.

    Orazio. My lord? my love! I am the Lord of Love;
So call me by my dukedom.——He has not?
We'll make him one, my nymph: when those bright eyes
Are closed, and that they shall not be, I swear,
'Till I have loved them many thousand hours,——
But when they are, their blue enchanted fire
Cupid shall take upon a torch of heaven,
And light the woody sides of some dim world,
Which shall be Bacchus' godson-star.
    Rosau.					Alas!
Their fire is but unsteady, weak and watery,
To guess by your love's wavering.
    Orazio.				Wine in a ruby!
I'll solemnize their beauty in a draught,
Pressed from the summer of an hundred vines.
Look on't, my sweet. Rosaura, this same night
I will immortalize those lips of thine,
That make a kiss so spicy. Touch the cup:
Ruby to ruby! Slave, let it be thrown,
At midnight, from a boat into mid-sea:
Rosaura's kiss shall rest unravished there,
While sea and land lie in each other's arms,
And curl the world.
    Batt.		Beggar, stand back, I say.
    Marc. No; I will shadow your adorèd mortal,
And shake my rags at him. Dost fear the plague?
Musk-fingered boy, aside!
    Orazio.				What madman's this?
    Rosau. Keep him away from me!
His hideous raggedness tears the soft sight,
Where it is pictured.

Marc. Your clutch is like the grasping of a wave:
Off from my shoulder!—Now, my velvet fellow,
Let's measure limbs. Well, is your flesh to mine
As gold to lead, or but the common plaister
That wraps up bones? Your skin is not of silk;
Your face not painted with an angel's feather
With tints from morning's lip, but the daubed clay;
These veiny pipes hold a dog's lap of blood.
Let us shake hands; I tell thee, brother skeleton,
We're but a pair of puddings for the dinner
Of Lady Worm; you served in silk and gems,
I garnished with plain rags. Have I unlocked thee?
  Orazio. Insolent beggar!
  Marc.   Prince! but we must shake hands.
Look you, the round earth's sleeping like a serpent,
Who drops her dusty tail upon her crown
Just here. Oh, we are like two mountain peaks,
Of two close planets, catching in the air;
You, King Olympus, a great pile of summer,
Wearing a crown of gods; I, the vast top
Of the ghosts' deadly world, naked and dark,
With nothing reigning on my desolate head
But one old spirit of a murdered god,
Palaced within the corpse of Saturn's father.
Then let's come near and hug. There's nothing like thee
But I thy contrast.—Thou'rt a prince, they say?
  Orazio. That you shall learn. You knaves, that wear
    my livery,
Will you permit me still to be defiled
By this worm's venom? Tread upon his neck,
And let's walk over him.

Marc.　　　　　　　Forbear, my lord!
I am a king of that most mighty empire,
That's built o'er all the earth, upon kings' crowns;
And poverty's its name; whose every hut
Stands on a coronet, or star, or mitre,
The glorious corner-stones.——But you are weary,
And would be playing with a woman's cheek:
Give me a purse then, prince.
　Orazio.　　　　　　No, not a doit:
The metal, I bestow, shall come in chains.
　Marc. Well, I can curse. Ay, prince, you have a
　　brother——
　Orazio. The Duke,——he'll scourge you.
　Marc.　　　　　　Nay, *the second*, sir,
Who, like an envious river, flows between
Your footsteps and Ferrara's throne.
　Orazio.　　　　　　He's gone:
Asia, and Africa, the sea he went on,
Have many mouths,——and in a dozen years,
(His absence' time,) no tidings or return,
Tell me We are but two.
　Marc. If he were in Ferrara——
　Orazio.　　　　Stood he before me there,
By you, in you,——as like as you're unlike,
Straight as you're bowed, young as you are old
And many years nearer than him to death,
The falling brilliancy of whose white sword
Your ancient locks so silverly reflect,——
I would deny, outswear, and overreach,
And pass him with contempt, as I do you.——
Jove! how we waste the stars: set on, my friends.

Batt. But the old ruffian?

Orazio.   Think of him to-morrow.
See, Venus rises in the softening heaven:
Let not your eyes abuse her sacred beams,
By looking through their gentleness on ought
But lips, and eyes, and blushes of dear love.

SONG

Strike, you myrtle-crownèd boys,
    Ivied maidens, strike together:
Magic lutes are these, whose noise
    Our fingers gather,
Threaded thrice with golden strings
    From Cupid's bow;
And the sounds of its sweet voice
Not air, but little busy things,
    Pinioned with the lightest feather
        Of his wings,
    Rising up at every blow
Round the chords, like flies from roses
Zephyr-touched; so these light minions
Hover round, then shut their pinions,
And drop into the air, that closes
Where music's sweetest sweet reposes.

[*Exit* ORAZIO *with his retinue*

Marc. (*solus*). Then who hath solitude, like mine,
    that is not
The last survivor of a city's plague,
Eating the mess he cooked for his dead father?
Who is alone but I? there's fellowship
In churchyards and in hell: but I!—no lady's ghost

Did ever cling with such a grasp of love
Unto its soft dear body, as I hung
Rooted upon this brother. I went forth
Joyfully, as the soul of one who closes
His pillowed eyes beside an unseen murderer,
And like its horrible return was mine,
To find the heart, wherein I breathed and beat,
Cold, gashed, and dead. Let me forget to love,
And take a heart of venom: let me make
A stair-case of the frightened breasts of men,
And climb into a lonely happiness!
And thou, who only art alone as I,
Great solitary god of that one sun,
I charge thee, by the likeness of our state,
Undo these human veins that tie me close
To other men, and let your servant griefs
Unmilk me of my mother, and pour in
Salt scorn and steaming hate!

Enter EZRIL

Ezr.   How now, my Lord?
Marc. Much better, my kind Jew. They've weeded
     out
A troublesome wild plant that grew upon me,
My heart: I've trampled it to dust, and wept it
Wetter than Nilus' side. Out of the sun!
And let him bake it to a wingèd snake.
—Well, you've been shouldered from the palace steps,
And spurned as I?—No matter.
Ezr.   Nay, my Lord!
Come with me: lay aside these squalid wrappings:

Prepare that honoured head to fit a crown,
For 'twill be empty of your brother soon.
    Marc. What starry chance has dropped out of the
      skies?
What's this? Oh! now if it should but be so,
I'll build a bridge to heaven. Tell me, good Jew;
Excellent Ezril, speak.
    Ezr.   At your command
I sought the ducal palace, and, when there,
Found all the wild-eyed servants in the courts
Running about on some dismaying errand,
In the wild manner of a market crowd,
Waked, from the sunny dozing at their stalls,
By one who cries "the city is on fire";
Just so they crossed, and turned, and came again.
I asked of an old man, what this might mean;
And he, yet grappling with the great disaster
As if he would have killed it, like a fable,
By unbelief, coldly, as if he spoke
Of something gone a century before,
Told me, the Duke in hunting had been thrown,
And lay on his last bed.
    Marc.   Ha! well! what next?
You are the cup-bearer of richest joy.—
But it was a report, a lie.—Have done—
I read it on your lip.
    Ezr.   It was too true.
I went to his bedside, and there made trial
Of my best skill in physic, with the zeal
Due to my sovereign.
    Marc.   Impious, meddling fool!

To thrust yourself 'twixt heaven and its victim!
Eʒr. My lord, I think you would not have said so
In the sad chamber of the writhing man.
He lay in a red fever's quenchless flames,
Burning to dust: despairing of my skill,
I sat myself beside his heart, and spoke
Of his next brother. When he heard of you,
He bade be summoned all his counsellors,
To witness his bequeathing his dominion
Wholly to you.
Marc.   Why did you let me wait?
Come let's be quick: he keeps beneath his pillow
A kingdom, which they'll steal if we're too late.
We must o'ertake his death.   [*Exeunt*

Aᛐ I

SCENE II

*   *   *

Oraʒio. No, it could not be so:—
I think and think—Sweet, did you like the feast?
Armida. Methought, 'twas gay enough.
Oraʒio. ·   Now, I did not.
'Twas dull: all men spoke slow and emptily.
Strange things were said by accident. Their tongues
Uttered wrong words: one fellow drank my death,
Meaning my health; another called for poison,
Instead of wine; and, as they spoke together,
Voices were heard, most loud, which no man owned:
There were more shadows too than there were men;
And all the air more dark and thick than night

Was heavy, as 'twere made of something more
Than living breaths.—
   Armida.   Nay, you are ill, my lord:
'Tis merely melancholy.
   Orazio.   There were deep hollows
And pauses in their talk: and then, again,
On tale, and song, and jest, and laughter rang,
Like a fiend's gallop. By my ghost, 'tis strange.—

        *   *   *

Exeunt MICHELE *and* ARMIDA *through the folding-door:* ORAZIO *is following them, but is stopped by the entry of an* Attendant, *from the side*

   Orazio.   What with you?
   Attend. A lady, in the garment of a nun,
Desires to see you.
   Orazio.   Lead her in: all such
I thank for their fair countenance.

Enter VALERIA [*her face veiled*], *introduced by* Attendant, *who withdraws*

                    Gentle stranger,
Your will with me?
   Valer. I am the bearer of another's will:
A woman, whose unhappy fondness yet
May trouble her lord's memory,—Valeria,—
Your's for a brief, blessed time, who now dwells
In her abandoned being patiently,
But not unsorrowing, sends me.
   Orazio.   My wrongéd wife!
Too purely good for such a man as I am!
If she remembers me, then Heaven does too,
And I am not yet lost. Give me her thoughts,—
Ay, the same words she put into thine ears,

Safe and entire, and I will thank thy lips
With my heart's thanks. But tell me how she fares.
  Valer. Well; though the common eye, that has a tear,
Would drop it for the paleness of her skin,
And the wan shivering of her torch of life;
Though she be faint and weak, yet very well:
For not the tincture, or the strength of limb,
Is a true health, but readiness to die.—
But let her be, or be not.—
  Orazio.   Best of ladies!
And, if thy virtues did not glut the mind,
To the extinction of the eye's desire,
Such a delight to see, that one would think
Our looks were thrown away on meaner things,
And given to rest on thee!
  Valer.   These words, my lord,
Are charitable; it is very kind
To think of her sometimes: for, day and night,
As they flow in and out of one another,
She sits beside and gazes on their streams,
So filled with the strong memory of you,
That all her outward form is penetrated,
Until the watery portrait is become
Not hers, but yours:—and so she is content
To wear her time out.
  Orazio.   Softest peace enwrap her!
Content be still the breathing of her lips!
Be tranquil ever, thou blest life of her!
And that last hour, that hangs 'tween heaven and earth,
So often travelled by her thoughts and prayers,
Be soft and yielding 'twixt her spirit's wings!

Valer. Think'st thou, Orazio, that she dies but once?
All round and through the spaces of creation,
No hiding-place of the least air, or earth,
Or sea, invisible, untrod, unrained on,
Contains a thing alone. Not e'en the bird,
That can go up the labyrinthine winds
Between its pinions, and pursues the summer,—
Not even the great serpent of the billows,
Who winds him thrice around this planet's waist,—
Is by itself, in joy or suffering.
But she whom you have ta'en, and, like a leaven,
With your existence kneaded, must be ever
Another—scarce another—self of thine.
    Orazio. If she has read her heart aloud to you,
Or you have found it open by some chance,
Tell me, dear lady, is my name among
Her paged secrets? does she, can she love me?—
No, no; that's mad:—does she remember me?
    Valer. She breathes away her weary days and nights
Among cold, hard-eyed men, and hides behind
A quiet face of woe: but there are things,—
A song, a face, a picture, or a word,—
Which, by some semblance, touch her heart to tears.
And music, starting up among the strings
Of a wind-shaken harp, undoes her secresy,—
Rolls back her life to the first starry hour
Whose flower-fed air you used, to speak of love;
And then she longs to throw her bursting breast,
And shut out sorrow with Orazio's arms,—
Thus,—O my husband!
    Orazio.   Sweetest, sweetest woman!

Valeria, thou dost squeeze eternity
Into this drop of joy. O come, come, come!
Let us not speak;—give me my wife again!—
O thou fair creature, full of my own soul!
We'll love, we'll love, like nothing under heaven,—
Like nought but Love, the very truest god.
Here's lip-room on thy cheek:—there, shut thine eye,
And let me come, like sleep, and kiss its lid.
Again.—What shall I do? I speak all wrong,
And lose a soul-full of delicious thought
By talking.—Hush! Let's drink each other up
By silent eyes. Who lives, but thou and I,
My heavenly wife?
   Valer.   Dear Orazio!
   Orazio. I'll watch thee thus, till I can tell a second
By thy cheek's change. O what a rich delight!
There's something very gentle in thy cheek,
That I have never seen in other women:
And, now I know the circle of thine eye,
It is a colour like to nothing else
But what it means,—that's heaven. This little tress,
Thou'lt give it me to look on and to wear,
But first I'll kiss its shadow on thy brow.
That little, fluttering dimple is too late,
If he is for the honey of thy looks:
As sweet a blush, as ever rose did copy,
Budded and opened underneath my lips,
And shed its leaves; and now these fairest cheeks
Are snowed upon them. Let us whisper, sweet,
And nothing be between our lips and ears
But our own secret souls.—   *[A horn without*

Valer.   Heaven of the blest, they're here!

Orazio. Who, what, Valeria?

Thou'rt pale and tremblest: what is it?

Valer.   Alas!

A bitter kernel to our taste of joy,

Our foolish and forgetful joy. My father!

Destruction, misery—

Enter VARINI *and attendants*

Varini.   Turn out those slaves,—

Burst the closed doors, and occupy the towers.—

   Orazio. Varini's self! what can his visit bring!

   Valer. Look there; he's walking hither like a man,

But is indeed a sea of stormy ruin,

Filling and flooding o'er this golden house

From base to pinnacle, swallowing thy lands,

Thy gold, thine all.—Embrace me into thee,

Or he'll divide us.

   Orazio.   Never! calm thyself.—

Now, Count Varini, what's your business here?

If as a guest, though uninvited, welcome!

If not, then say, what else?

   Varini.   A master, spendthrift!

Open those further doors,—

   Orazio.   What? in my palace!

   Varini. Thine! what is thine beneath the night or day?

Not e'en that beggar's carcase,—for within that

The swinish devils of filthy luxury

Do make their stye.—No lands, no farms, no houses,—

Thanks to thy debts, no gold. Go out! Thou'rt nothing,

Besides a grave and a deep hell.

Valer.   Orazio,
Thou hast Valeria: the world may shake thee off,
But thou wilt drop into this breast, this love,—
And it shall hold thee.
    Orazio.   What? lost already!
O that curst steward! I have fallen, Valeria,
Deeper than Lucifer, though ne'er so high,—
Into a place made underneath all things,
So low and horrible that hell's its heaven.
    Varini. Thou shalt not have the idiot, though she be
The very fool and sickness of my blood.—
Gentlemen, here are warrants for my act,—
His debts, bonds, forfeitures, taxes and fines,
O'erbalancing the worth of his estates,
Which I have bought: behold them!—For the girl,
Abandoned, after marriage, by the villain,—
I am her father: let her be removed;
And, if the justice of my rightful cause
Ally you not, at least do not resist me.
    Michele. What are these writings?
    Batt.   Bills under the Duke's seal,
All true and valid.—Poor Orazio!
    Orazio. Why, the rogue pities me! I'm down indeed.
    Valer. Help me! Oh! some of you have been
    beloved,
Some must be married.—Will you let me go?
Will you stand frozen there, and see them cut
Two hearts asunder?—Then you will,—you do.—
Are all men like my father? are all fathers
So far away from men? or all their sons
So heartless?—you are women, as I am;

Then pity me, as I would pity you,
And pray for me! Father! ladies! friends!—
But you are tearless as the desert sands.—
Orazio, love me! or, if thou wilt not,
Yet I will love thee: that you cannot help.

 Orazio. My best Valeria! never shalt thou leave me,
But with my life. O that I could put on
These feeble arms the proud and tawny strength
Of the lion in my heart!

 Varini.   Out with the girl at once!

 Rosaur. Forgive them, sir, we all of us beseech.

 Varini. Lady, among you all she's but one sire,
And he says *no.*—Away!

 Valer. Have pity, my sweet father! my good father!
Have pity, as my gentle mother would,
Were she alive,—thy sainted wife! O pardon,
If I do wish you had been rent asunder,
Thus dreadfully; for then I had not been;—
Not kissed and wept upon my father's hand,
And he denied me!—you can make me wretched:—
Be cruel still, but I will never hate you.—
Orazio, I'll tell thee what it is:
The world is dry of love; we've drunk it all
With our two hearts—

 Orazio.   Farewell, Valeria!
Take on thy lost dear hand this truest kiss,
Which I have brought thee from my deepest soul.—
Farewell, my wife!—

 Valer.   They cannot part us long.—
What's life? our love is an eternity:
O blessed hope!   [*She is forced out*

Orazio. Now, then, sir; speak to me:
The rest is sport,—like rain against a tower
Unpalsied by the ram. Go on: what's next?
Varini. Your palaces are mine, your sheep-specked
pastures,
Forest and yellow corn land, grove and desart,
Earth, water, wealth: all, that you yesterday
Were mountainously rich and golden with,
I, like an earthquake, in this minute take.
Go, go: I will not pick thee to the bones:
Starve as you will.
Orazio. How, sir! am I not wealthy?
Why, if the sun could melt the brazen man
That strode o'er Corinth, and whose giant form
Stretched its swart limbs along sea, island, mountain,
While night appeared its shadow,—if *he* could,—
Great, burning Phoebus' self—could melt ought of him,
Except the snowdrift on his rugged shoulder,
Thou hast destroyèd *me*!
Varini. Thanks to these banquets of Olympus' top
From whence you did o'erturn whole Niles of wine,
And made each day as rainy as that hour
When Perseus was begot, I have destroyed thee,
Or thou thyself; for, such a luxury
Would wring the gold out of its rocky shell,
And leave the world all hollow.—So, begone;
My lord, and beggar!
Batt. Noble, old Varini,
Think, is it fit to crush into the dirt
Even the ruins of nobility?
Take comfort, sir.

Orazio.   Who am I now?
How long is a man dying or being born?
Is't possible to be a king and beggar
In half a breath? or to begin a minute
I' th' west, and end it in the furthest east?
O no! I'll not believe you. When I do,
My heart will crack to powder.—Can you speak?
Then do: shout something louder than my thoughts,
For I begin to feel.   [*Enter a* Messenger

Mess.   News from the court:
The Duke—

Orazio.   My brother—speak—
Was he not ill, and on a perilous bed?
Speak life and death,—thou hast them on thy tongue,—
One's mine, the other his:—a look, a word,
A motion;—life or death?

Mess.   The Duke is dead.

BATTISTA *and the other guests kneel to* ORAZIO

Batt. Then we salute in thee another sovereign.
Orazio. Me then, who just was shaken into chaos,
Thou hast created! I have flown, somehow,
Upwards a thousand miles: my heart is crowned.—
Your hands, good gentlemen; sweet ladies, yours:—
And what new godson of the bony death,—
Of fire, or steel, or poison,—shall I make
For old Varini?

Varini.   Your allegiance, sirs,
Wanders: Orazio is a beggar still.

Batt. Is it not true then that the Duke is dead?
Orazio. Not dead? O slave!

Varini.   The Duke is dead, my lords;
And, on his death-bed, did bestow his crown
Upon his second brother, Lord Marcello,—
Ours, and Ferrara's, Duke.
    Orazio.   I'll not believe it:
Marcello is abroad.
    Varini.   His blest return,
This providential day, has saved our lives
From thine abhorrèd sway. Orazio, go:
And, though my clemency is half a crime,
I spare your person.
    Orazio.   I'll to the palace.
When we meet next, be blessed if thou dost kiss
The dust about my ducal chair.   [*Exit*
    Varini.   I shall be there,
To cry Long live Marcello! in thine ear.—
Pray pardon me the breaking of this feast,
Ladies,—and so, good-night.
    Rosaur. Your wish is echoed by our inmost will:
Good night to Count Varini.   [*Exeunt guests*
    Attend.   My lord—
    Varin. What are they, sirrah?
    Attend.   The palace-keys.
There is a banquet in the inner room:
Shall we remove the plate?
    Varini.   Leave it alone:
Wine in the cups, the spicy meats uncovered,
And the round lamps each with a star of flame
Upon their brink; let winds begot on roses,
And grey with incense, rustle through the silk
And velvet curtains:—then set all the windows,

The doors and gates, wide open; let the wolves,
Foxes, and owls, and snakes, come in and feast;
Let the bats nestle in the golden bowls,
The shaggy brutes stretch on the velvet couches,
The serpent twine him o'er and o'er the harp's
Delicate chords:—to Night, and all its devils,
We do abandon this accursed house.   [*Exeunt*

Aɛt II

SCENE I. *An apartment in Varini's palace*

*   *   *

Valer.   Innocently thought,
And worthy of thy youth! I should not say
How thou art like the daisy in Noah's meadow,
On which the foremost drop of rain fell warm
And soft at evening; so the little flower
Wrapped up its leaves, and shut the treacherous water
Close to the golden welcome of its breast,—
Delighting in the touch of that which led
The shower of oceans, in whose billowy drops
Tritons and lions of the sea were warring,
And sometimes ships on fire sunk in the blood
Of their own inmates; others were of ice,
And some had islands rooted in their waves,
Beasts on their rocks, and forest-powdering winds,
And showers tumbling on their tumbling self,—
And every sea of every ruined star
Was but a drop in the world-melting flood.—
    Attend. Lady, you utter dreams.
    Valer.   Let me talk so:

I would o'erwhelm myself with any thoughts;
Ay, hide in madness from the truth. Persuade me
To hope that I am not a wretched woman,
Who knows she has a husband by his absence,
Who feels she has a father by his hate,
And wakes and mourns, imprisoned in this house,
The while she should be sleeping, mad, or dead.
Thou canst, and pity on thine eyelid hangs,
Whose dewy silence drops consent,—thou wilt!
I've seen thee smile with calm and gradual sweetness,
As none, that were not good, could light their cheeks:—
Thou wilt assist me. Harden not those lips,
Those lovely kissings let them not be stone
With a denial!
    Attend.   But your father's anger,—
The watchful faith of all the servants—
    Valer.   Fear not:
Lend me thy help. O come,—I see thou wilt.—
Husband, I'll lay me on thine aching breast
For once and ever.—Haste! for see, the light
Creates for earth its day once more, and lays
The star of morn's foundation in the east.
Come—Come—   [*Exeunt*

Act II

SCENE II. *Place before the ducal palace*

Guards driving ORAZIO *from the gate*

Guard. Back! desperate man: you cannot pass—
Orazio. By heaven, I must and will:—
Guard. By the Duke's order,

The gates are locked on all to-day.

   Orazio.   By mine,
By the Duke's brother's order, or his force,
Open at once yon gates. Slave, by my blood,
But that I think thou know'st me not, I'd make
That corpse of thine my path. Undo, I say,
The knitting of this rebel house's arms,
And let their iron welcome be around me.
My sword is hungry: do't.

   Guard.   Advance no further:
Another step, and all our swords shake hands
Within your breast.

   Orazio.   Insolent worm of earth,
To earth and worms for this!   *[He draws his sword*

   Guard.   Strike all! strike strong!
Strike through him right.   *[They fight*

Enter EZRIL *from the palace*

   Ezr.   Peace, on your lives, you traitors!
What! would you stain the holy throne of justice,
The pure and peaceful temple of the law,
The sacred dwelling of Ferrara's soul,
With the foul juices of your drunken veins?
Put up your impious swords.

   Guard. Pardon our hasty and forgetful choler:
We but defend our Duke against the outrage
Of this intemperate brawler.

   Orazio. Cut him to shreds and fling him to the dogs.—
You wait upon the Duke, sir?

   Ezr.   I am one
Of Lord Marcello's followers.

Orazio.   Pray you then,
Speak to your Lord Marcello: let him know
These house-dogs, these his ducal latch-holders
Dare keep the bolt against his brother's knock.

   Ezr. Are you then—?

   Orazio.   I am Lord Orazio.—
Be quick!—O nature, what a snail of men!
The morn is frosty, sir: I love not waiting.—

   Ezr. Now all the mercy of the heavens forbid
That thou should'st be that rash and wretched neigh-
    bour
Of the Duke's crown, his brother!

   Orazio. Marcello is my brother; I am his;
If coming of one mother brother us:
He is the Duke, and I Orazio;
He elder, younger I.—If Jove and Neptune,
And the third Pluto, being Saturn's boys,
Lying in Rhea's womb and on her breast,
Were therefore brethren, so are he and I,—
Marcello's mother's son, his grandame's grandson,
Marcello's father's babe, his uncle's nephew,
His nephew's uncle, brother of his brother,
Or what you like,—if this same word of brother,
Sours the sore palate of a royal ear.

   Ezr. Better thou wert the brother of his foe
Than what thou art, a man of the same getting;
As, out of the same lump of sunny Nile,
Rises a purple-wingèd butterfly,
And a cursed serpent crawls.

   Orazio. Heart-withered, pale-scalped grandfather of
    lies!

Age-hidden monster! Tell me what thou meanest,
And then I'll stab thee for thy falsehood.

Ezr. Hold him!
Your swords between us!—Now, the Duke condemns
    thee;
And by his mother's, and his father's grave,
And by the dead, that lies within this palace,
His brother's sacred corpse, he dreadly swears;
And by the heaven those three loved souls
Dwell and are blest in, twice he dreadly swears:
By which dread oath, and hate of all thy crimes,
The Duke condemns thee,—mixing in his sentence,
Sweet mercy, tearful love, and justice stern,—
To banishment for ever from this hour.

Orazio. O reddest hour of wrath and cruelty!
Banished!—Why not to death?

Ezr.   The pious hope,
That bitter solitude and suffering thought
Will introduce repentance to thy woes,
And that conduct thee to religious fear
And humbleness, the lark that climbs heaven's stairs
But lives upon the ground:—Go forth, Orazio;
Seek not the house or converse of a citizen,
But think thyself outside the walls of life:
If in Ferrara, after this decree,
Your darkest, deepest, and most fearful fear
Falls on thy shoulder, digs beneath thy feet,
And opens hell for thee.—So, pass away!

Orazio. Stay, for an instant; listen to a word:
O lead me to his throne! Let me but look
Upon the father in my brother's face!

Let me but speak to him this kindred voice,
Our boyish thoughts in the familiar words
Of our one bed-room; let me show to him
That picture which contains our double childhood,
Embracing in inexplicable love,
Within each other's, in our mother's arms;
Thou'lt see rejoicing, O thou good old man,
The rigour melting through his changèd eyes
Off his heart's roots, between whose inmost folds
Our love is kept.

  Ezr.   Impossible and vain!
Content thee with thy doom, and look for love
Over the sea-wide grave. Let us be gone!

            [*Exit with guards*

 Orazio. Let me write to him,—send a message to
   him,—
A word, a touch, a token! old, benevolent man,
Stay with me then to comfort and advise:
Leave one of these beside me: throw me not
Alone into despair!—He's gone; they're gone;
They never will come back; ne'er shall I hear
The sweet voice of my kinsmen or my friends:
But here begins the solitude of death.
I was,—I am; O what a century
Of darkness, rocks, and ghostly tempest opens
Between those thoughts! Within it there are lost
Dearest Valeria,—Marcello, whose heart came
From the same place as mine,—and all mankind;
Affection, charity, joy; and nothing's cast
Upon this barren rock of present time,
Except Orazio's wreck! here let it lie.

          [*Throws himself down*

Enter VARINI *and attendants*

Varini. Not in the city? Have you asked the guards
At bridge and gate,—the palace sentinels?

Attend. We have,—in vain: they have not seen her
pass.

Varini. And did you say Valeria,—my Valeria,—
Heaven's love,—earth's beauty?

Orazio. (*starting up*). Mine eternally!
Let heaven unscabbard each star-hilted lightning,
And clench ten thousand hands at once against me,—
Earth shake all graves to one, and rive itself
From Lybia to the North! in spite of all
That threatens, I will stun the adulterous gods,—
She's mine! Valeria's mine! dash me to death,—
From death to the eternal depth of fire,—
I laugh and triumph on the neck of fate:
For still she's mine for ever! give me her,
Or I will drag thee to a sea-side rock,
That breaks the bottoms of the thunder-clouds,
And taking thee by this old, wicked hair,
Swing thee into the winds.—

Varini.   I would, wild man,
That I could quench thine eyes' mad thirst with her.
She's gone, fled, lost. O think not any more—
Let us forget what else is possible,—
Yea hope impossibly! the city streets,
The quay, the gardens,—is there yet a place
Within night's skirt unsearched?

Orazio.   The wood of wolves:—

Varini. Merciful god! that frightful forest grows
Under the darksome corner of the sky

Where death's scythe hangs: its murder-shading trees
Are hairs upon Hell's brow. Away: away!
And never dare to turn on me again
Those eyes, unfilled with—speak to me never,
Until you cry—"Behold Valeria!"
And drop her on my bosom.
    Orazio. We'll wind the gordian paths off the trees'
      roots,
Untie the hilly mazes, and seek her
Till we are lost. Help, ho!   [*Exit with attendants*
    Varini.   Blessings of mine
Feather your speed! and my strong prayers make
    breaches
Through the air before you!   [*He sits down on the palace-step*
                        Now I'll close my eyes,
And, seated on this step, await their coming.
Strange and delightful meetings, on strange lands,
Of dead-esteemèd friends have happened oft,
And such a blessèd and benevolent chance
Might bring her here unheard; for on the earth
She goes with her light feet, still as the sparrow
Over the air, or through the grass its shade.
Behind me would she steal, unknown, until
Her lip fell upon mine. It might be so:
I'll wait awhile and hope it.

Enter VALERIA

    Valer. I know not what it means. None speak to me:
The crowded street, and solid flow of men,
Dissolves before my shadow and is broken.
I pass unnoticed, though they search for me,

As I were in the air and indistinct
As crystal in a wave. There lies a man:—
Shall I intreat protection and concealment,
And thaw the pity of his wintry head?
—No time: they come like arrows after me:—
I must avoid them.   [*Exit*

Enter EZRIL *and attendants*

   Ezr. Pursue, o'ertake, stay, seize that hurrying girl:
Muffle her face and form, and through the bye-ways
Convey her to the palace. Hasten, hounds!   [*Exeunt*
   Varini. Thou magical deceiver, precious Fancy!
Even now, out of this solitude and silence,
Seemed,—it was thy creation,—music flowing,
And a conviction of some unseen influence;
I could have pointed to that empty spot,
And said, there stands the presence of my daughter!
The air seemed shaken by that voice of hers,—
But 'tis all hushed.   [*Some of his attendants return*
                     How now? speak some of you.
What's here?
   Attend.   A veil and mantle.—
   Varini.   Both Valeria's!
Where's she they should have wrapped?
   Attend.   'Twas all we found.
   Varini. Where?
   Attend. On the grass this purple cloak was dropped,
Beside the river.
   Varini.   And the veil,—which way?
Further on the shore, or near those deadly waves?
   Attend. The veil, my lord,—

Varini. 'Tis drenched and dropping wet:
Would I were drowned beside her! thou wert white;
And thy limbs' wond'rous victory over snow
Did make the billows thirsty to possess them.
They drank thee up, thou sweet one, cruelly!
Who was in heaven then?

Enter ORAZIO *and attendants, bearing a corpse that
is carried up the stage*

Orazio. My love, art dead?
Wilt thou not ope thy lips, lift up thine eyes?
It is the air, the sun—
Attend. (to Varini). We've found the corpse.
Orazio. Her corpse! O no! she is Valeria still:
She's scarce done living yet: her ghost's the youngest!
To-morrow she'll be—Oh what *she* will be?
No she,—a corpse, and then—a skeleton!—
Varini. Hast looked upon her?
Attend. Death has marred her features,—
So swollen and discoloured their delight,
As if he feared that Life should know her sweet one,
And take her back again.
Varin. If it be so,
I'll see her once: that beauty being gone,
And the familiar tokens altered quite,
She's strange,—a being made by wicked Death,
And I'll not mourn her. Lead me to the corpse.
[*Exit with attendants*

Orazio. Henceforth, thou tender pity of mankind,
Have nought to do with weeping: let war's eyes
Sweat with delight; and tears be ta'en from grief,

And thrown upon the rocky cheek of hate!
For mark! that water, the soft heap of drops,—
Water, that feigns to come from very heaven
In the round shape of sorrow,—that was wont to wash
Sin from the new-born babe, is hard and bloody;
A murderer of youth; cold death to those
Whose life approved thy godhead, piteous virtue!

Enter EZRIL *and guards*

Ezr. Here still, unhappy man? then take the doom
You woo so obstinately.—To the dungeon,—
To the deepest chamber of the dayless rock:
Away, and down with him!
    Orazio.   I care not whither.
Thou canst not drag me deeper, wrap me darker,
Or torture me as my own thoughts have done.   [*Exeunt*

Act III

SCENE I. *A room in the ducal palace*

MARCELLO *alone*

Marc. I have them all at last; swan-necked Obedience;
And Power that strides across the muttering people,
Like a tall bridge; and War, the spear-maned dragon:—
Such are the potent spirits he commands,
Who sits within the circle of a crown!
Methought that love began at woman's eye:
But thou, bright imitation of the sun,
Kindlest the frosty mould around my heart-roots,
And, breathing through the branches of my veins,
Makest each azure tendril of them blossom
Deep, tingling pleasures, musically hinged,

Dropping with starry sparks, goldenly honied,
And smelling sweet with the delights of life.
At length I am Marcello.

Enter EZRIL

E{r.   Mighty Duke,
Ferrara's nobles wait on you, to proffer
The homage of their coronets.
    Marc.   I shall not see them.
    E{r. It was the ancient usage of the state,
In every age.—
    Marc.   Henceforth, be it forgotten!
I will not let the rabble's daily sight
Be my look's playmate. Say unto them, Ezril,
Their sovereigns of foretime were utter men,
False gods, that beat an highway in their thoughts
Before my car; idols of monarchy,
Whose forms they might behold. Now I am come,
Be it enough that they are taught my name,
Permitted to adore it, swear and pray
In it and to it; for the rest I wrap
The pillared caverns of my palace round me,
Like to a cloud, and rule invisibly
On the god-shouldering summit of mankind.
Dismiss them so.
    E{r.   'Tis dangerous,—
    Marc.   Begone!
Each minute of man's safety he does walk
A bridge, no thicker than his frozen breath,
O'er a precipitous and craggy danger
Yawning to death!   [*Exit* EZRIL

A perilous sea it is,
'Twixt this and Jove's throne, whose tumultuous waves
Are heaped, contending ghosts! There is no passing,
But by those slippery, distant stepping-stones,
Which frozen Odin trod, and Mahomet,
With victories harnessed to his crescent sledge,
And building waves of blood upon the shallows,
O'erpassed triumphant: first a pile of thrones
And broken nations, then the knees of men,
From whence, to catch the lowest root of heaven,
We must embrace the winged waist of fame,
Or nest within opinion's palmy top
'Till it has mixed its leaves with Atlas's hair,
Quicker to grow than were the men of Cadmus—

Re-enter EZRIL

Ezr. They are departing, with the unequal pace
Of discontent and wonder.
Marc.   Send them home
To talk it with their wives: sow them with books
Of midnight marvels, witcheries, and visions:
Let the unshaven Nazarite of stars
Unbind his wondrous locks, and grandame's earthquake
Drop its wide jaw; and let the church-yard's sleep
Whisper out goblins. When the fools are ripe
And gaping to the kernel, thou shalt steal,
And lay the egg of my divinity
In their fermenting sides.—Where is my brother?
The first I'll aim at.
Ezr. 'Mid the poisonous dregs of this deep building,
Two days and their two nights have had his breath

All of one colour to his darkened eyes.
No voice has fed his ears, and little food
His speech-robbed lips.
    Marc.   'Tis well. This is a man
Whose state has sunk i' th' middle of his thoughts:
And in their hilly shade, as in a vale,
I'll build my church, making his heart the quarry.
Take him his meal, and place a guard around
The wood below: the rest of my instructions,
For we must juggle boldly, shall be whispered
Secretly in my closet.
    Ezr.   Will you not
First cast this ragged and unseemly garb,
And hang your sides with purple?
    Marc.   No: these rags
Give my delight a sting. I'll sit in them;
And, when I've stretched my dukedom through men's
    souls,
Fix on its shore my chair, and from it bid
Their doubts lie down.—Wilt help me?
    Ezr.   Duke, thou art
A fathomless and undiscovered man,
Thinking above the eagle's highest wings,
And underneath the world. Go on: command:
And I am thine to do.   [*Exeunt*

       SCENE II. *A dungeon of Cyclopean architecture:*
            ORAZIO *lying on the ground*

    Orazio. I'll speak again:
This rocky wall's great silence frightens me,
Like a dead giant's.

Methought I heard a sound; but all is still.
This empty silence is so deadly low,
The very stir and winging of my thoughts
Make audible my being: every sense
Aches from its depth with hunger.
The pulse of time is stopped, and night's blind sun
Sheds its black light, the ashes of noon's beams,
On this forgotten tower, whose ugly round,
Amid the fluency of brilliant morn,
Hoops in a blot of parenthetic night,
Like ink upon the crystal page of day,
Crossing its joy! But now some lamp awakes,
And, with the venom of a basilisk's wink,
Burns the dark winds. Who comes?

Enter EZRIL

Ezr.   There's food for thee.
Eat heartily; be mirthful with your cup;
Though coarse and scanty.
Orazio.   I'll not taste of it.
To the dust, to the air with the cursed liquids
And poison-kneaded bread.
Ezr.   Why dost thou this?
Orazio. I know thee and thy master: honey-lipped,
Viper-tongued villain, that dost bait intents,
As crook'd and murderous as the scorpion's sting,
With mercy's sugared milk, and poisonest
The sweetest teat of matron charity!

Enter MARCELLO

Marc. Thou hast her then, in secret and secure?
Ezr. Not firmer or more quietly this body
Holds its existing spirit.

Marc.   Excellent Ezril!
Thanks, thanks: my gratitude is snail-paced slow,
So heavy is its burthen.—See'st thou yonder?
  Ezr. The husband: where his sorrow, strong in error,
Has spurned him down.
  Marc.   I'll raise the broken man:
Ay, I will place my foot upon his soul,
And weigh him up.—Leave us alone, good Ezril.—
                                    [*Exit* EZRIL

          *   *   *

  Orazio. Thou talk'st to me of spirits and of souls:—
What are they? what know I or you of them?
I love no ghost: I love the fairest woman,
With too much warmth and beauty in her cheek,
And gracious limbs, to hold together long.
To-day she's cold and breathless, and to-morrow
They'll lay her in the earth; there she will crumble;
Another year no place in all the world,
But this poor heart, will know of her existence.
Can she come back, O can she ever be
The same she was last night in my embrace?
No comfort else, no life!

          *   *   *

Act IV

SCENE I. *The Campo Santo. Night*

*   *   *

Valer.   I have a plea,
As dewy-piteous as the gentle ghost's
That sits alone upon a forest-grave,
Thinking of no revenge: I have a mandate,
As magical and potent as e'er ran
Silently through a battle's myriad veins,
Undid their fingers from the hanging steel,
And drew them up in prayer: I AM A WOMAN.
O motherly remembered be the name,
And, with the thought of loves and sisters, sweet
And comforting! Therefore be piteous to me.
O let my hand touch yours! I could do more
By its sad tremors than my tongue.
     Melchior.   Away!
We own a mood of marble. There's no earth
In any crevice of my well-built spirit,
Whence woman's rain could wake the weedy leaves
Of the eye-poison, pity.
     Marc.   If I were
Another man than this, Nature's cast child,
Renounced by Life and Death of common men,
And placed by wrongs upon an island-peak,
Methinks I could relent.
     Melchior.   Draw up thyself.
This bearskin, charity, is a great coat
For ragged, shivering sin: thine Indian hate,

That shivers, like the serpent's noontide tongue,
With poisonous, candid heat, must trample on it.

* * *

[*Unfinished in the original*]

Aȼt IV

SCENE II

Enter EZRIL *dragged in by two Venetians*

Eʒr. Help! help, you kindly people of this place!
Help for the helpless old! Have mercy, sirs!
Oh! it is in your hearts, deny it not;
Shut not your ears to its enchanting tongue.
It will unlock a heaven in your souls,
Wherein my pardon and my pity sits.
I kneel to you, as you unto your god:
Reject me not, teach him not cruelty.
Be heavenly, as you can.
    1*st Venet.*   Hush! frosty Jew!
Or take my answer from this tongue of steel.
    Eʒr. When you are old, and fearful,
With age's wintry winds shaking your limbs,
Thus may you cry, thus may you wring your hands,—
    1*st Venet.* And thus be struck. Once more have
    silence with thee,
Or death possess me if I stab thee not.
Now comrade, shall we let the coward live?
    2*nd Venet.* Wilt thou betray us, dotard?
    Eʒr.   By my life,
If you will grant me it to swear upon,
Never!

1st Venet. It is a rubbed and brittle oath,
As what 'tis sworn: break one, thou breakest both.
I'll snap thy being like a frozen breath,
If thou breathest falsely.

Ezr.   If I kill my truth,
Drive thy revenge into my midmost heart.

1st Venet. Hark, once again! Where wert thou
    journeying, Jew,
With gold-stuffed panniers, thus?

Ezr.   To Venice town.—
Alas! remind me not of my dear riches,
The beauteous jewels of my bosom; take them.—
I would that I were stouter in my soul,
That I dared die!—Be gentle with the sacks;
They're full of fair, white silver: as I tied them,
I felt their strings run tickling through my veins.

1st Venet. O ho! here's royal booty, on my soul:
A draught of ducats! By this silver sight
I love thee, bushy dog, and thou shalt live
To sweep the corners of men's souls again.
Be comforted. Let's toss them on our shoulders,
And swim the Po.

2nd Venet.   First, look you here, old man:
There's a clenched hand; dost see?

Ezr.   'Tis hard as iron:
(*Aside*) Hell melt it so!

2nd Venet.   And in't a sword:—

Ezr. (*aside*). As sharp as are the teeth
Of my heart's father, a fierce curse of thee.—
What then, sir?

2nd Venet. Speak once of us,

Look after us, or press that foot of thine
Upon yon lip of Po, where Venice grows,—
They're in thy muddy body to the wrist.

[Exeunt Venetians

Eʒr. The weight of Atlas' shoulder slip upon you!
The waves smile, do they? O, that they would laugh,
Open their liquid jaws and shut them on you!
These are but thieves, the emptiers of my soul,—
These, that have scooped away my sweetest kernel,
My gathered seed of kingdom-shading wealth,
Crown-blossomed, sword-leaved, trunked with
        struggling armies,
And left the wrinkled skin upon my arms,—
These are but thieves! And he that steals the blood,
A murderer is he? Oh! my thoughts are blunt:—
I'll throw away the workings of my tongue,
Till I've the craft to make a curse so long,
Fangish enough to reach the quick of earth,
That hell whose flaming name my feelings echo,
And rouse it for them.
                    Death! here comes a man
To stare into my ruin.

Enter MARCELLO

Marc.   Hail, country of my birth
We're met in season; winter in us both,
The fruit picked from us, poor and snowy-scalped,
And almost solitary. I did turn
An ermined shoulder on thee, when I stepped
Out of thine airy door of earth and sky,
Upon that watery threshold;

And now I face thee with a ragged front:
A coin of Fate's cross-stamp, that side a Duke,
And this, which Time turns up (so hell might stick
Upon the back of heaven,) a scratched despair!

*   *   *

[*Here the play breaks off.*]

TORRISMOND

PERSONS REPRESENTED

DUKE OF FERRARA
TORRISMOND; *his son*
The Marquis MALASPINA
CYRANO; *his son*
AMADEUS; *a young nobleman*
GARCIA;
GOMEZ; } *Duke's servants*
ORAN;
MELCHIOR; } *Courtiers*
GAUDENTIO;
VERONICA [*Malaspina's daughter*]
ELVIRA; *a toad-eater*
ERMINIA; *Oran's sister*

SCENE: Ferrara

Act I

SCENE I. *An apartment in the ducal palace*

Enter the DUKE, *Courtiers, and attendants*

Duke. Who has seen Torrismond, my son, to-night?
Garcia. My lord, he has not crossed me, all the day.
(*To Gomez aside*). You need not say we saw him pass
    the terrace,
All red and hot with wine. The duke is angry:
Mark how he plucks his robe.
    Duke.   Gomez, nor you?
    Gomez. Your Grace in Garcia's answer
Beheld the face of mine. I have not lent him
A word to-day.

Duke.   Nor you? none of you, sirs?—
No answer! have ye sold yourselves to silence?
Is there not breath, or tongue, or mouth among you,
Enough to croak a curse?—Nay: there's no wonder.
Why do I ask? that know you are his curs,
His echo-birds, the mirrors of his tongue.
He has locked up this answer in your throats,
And scratched it on your leaden memories.
What do I ask for? Well: go on, go on;
Be his sop-oracles, and suck yellow truth
Out of the nipple of his jingling pouch.
But tell me this, dogs, that do wag your tails
Round this dwarf Mercury, this gilded Lie-god,
Will you set out and beg with him to-morrow?
    Garcia. Why, my good lord?
    Duke.   Because, my evil slave,—
Because unless he can these sunbeams coin,
Or, like a bee in metals, suck me out
The golden honey from their marly core,
He's like to board with the cameleon:
Because I will untie him from my heart,
And drop him to the bottom of the world:—
Because I'll melt his wings.—Enough!
    Garcia.   With pardon,
You are too rough.—
    Duke.   Too rough! were I as loud
As shaggy Boreas in his bearish mood,—
Did I roll wheels of thunder o'er your souls,
And break them into groans,—weep yourselves waves,
And kneel beneath my storming. Worms ye are,
Born in the fat sides of my pouring wealth:—

Lie there and stir not, or I dash you off.

   Garcia. My lord—

   Duke.   I am no lord, sir, but a father:

My son has stuck sharp injuries in my heart,

And flies to hide in your obscurity.

Cover him not with falsehoods; shield him not;

Or, by my father's ashes,—but no matter.

You said I was a duke: I will be one,

Though graves should bark for it. You've heard me
    speak:

Now go not to your beds until my son

(—It is a word that cases not a meaning,—)

Come from his riots: send him then to me:

And hark! ye fill him not, as ye are wont,

To the lip's brim with oily subterfuges.—

I sit this evening in the library.

   An attend. Lights, lights there for the duke!

   Duke. For the duke's soul I would there were a
    light!

Well; on thy flinty resolution strike,

Benighted man! The sun has laid his hair

Up in that stone, as I have treasured love

In a cold heart;—but it begins to boil,

And, if it breaks its casket, will be out.

Find me a book of fables: he, whose world

Grows in his thoughts, methinks, alone is happy.

So now good-night; and do as I have said.

   Garcia. We shall.—Good dreams, your Grace!

   Duke. Good acts, you mean.

He who does ill, awake, and turns to night

For lovely painted shades,

Is like a satyr grinning in a brook
To find Narcissus' round and downy cheek.

Exit with attendants: manent GARCIA *and* GOMEZ

Gomez. I never saw my lord so sad and angry:
His blood foamed, white with wrath, beneath his face,
Rising and falling like a sea-shore wave.
What boils him thus?
Garcia.　　　　　　　Perhaps some further outrage
Reported of his son; for the young lord,
Whose veins are stretched by passion's hottest wine,
Tied to no law except his lawless will,
Ranges and riots headlong through the world;—
Like a young dragon, on Hesperian berries
Purplely fed, who dashes through the air,
Tossing his wings in gambols of desire,
And breaking rain-clouds with his bulging breast.
Thus has he been from boy to youth and manhood,
Reproved, then favoured; threatened, next forgiven;
Renounced, to be embraced: but, till this hour,
Never has indignation like to this,
With lightning looks, black thoughts, and stony words,
Burst o'er the palace of their love, which stretches
From heart to heart.
Gomez.　　　　　　I fear that both will shake;
And that fair union, built by interchange
Of leaning kindnesses, in the recoil
May fall between, and leave no bridge for pardon.
Garcia. The little that we can, then let us strive
To hold them in the lock of amity:
For which our thoughts let us compare within.

[*Exeunt*

SCENE II. *A banqueting room in Malaspina's palace*

CYRANO, AMADEUS, TORRISMOND, *and other young lords, drinking*

Amad. Another health! Fill up the goblets, sirrah!
This wine was pressed from full and rolling grapes
By the white dance of a Circassian princess,
Whose breast had never aught but sunlight touched,
And her own tears: 'tis spicy, cool, and clear
As is a magic fount where rainbows grow,
Or nymphs by moonlight bathe their tremulous limbs;
And works an intellectual alchemy,
Touching the thoughts to sunshine. Now, to whom,—
To what young saint, between whose breathing paps
Love's inspiration lies,—shall we devote
This last and richest draught: with whose soft name
Shall we wash bright our hearts? Say, Cyrano.

Cyrano. Let Torrismond be sponsor for this bowl.
He sate so still last night, that by plump Cupid,
That merry, cherry-lipped, delicious god,
Whose name is writ on roses, I must think
He's paid away his soul in broken sighs,
Glass oaths, and tears of crocodilish coinage,
For one quick finger-kiss. Ask him, what name,
Made to be written upon hearts and trees,
And grace a sonnet, shall be sugar here,
Making the juice steam music.

Torris.   I beseech you,
Waste not this Araby of words on me:
I'm dull, but not in love.

Cyrano.   Not ancle-deep?
What means a leaning head, eyelids ajar,

And lips thick-sown with whispers? Sir, I say,
Before to-morrow you'll be soused in love,
To the ear's tip. In truth, it will be so;
Sure as an almanac.

    Torris.   I lay my fate
Upon your mercy: e'en tie love-knots in it,
If you've nought else to do. Good Cyrano,
And you, sirs, all pray drink. I fear the fog
Of my most stupid dulness spreads.

    Amad.   We'll drink
One cup,—one more liquid delight, my friends;
Then for the masquerade at Signor Paulo's.—

    Cyrano. Ay; dedicated to the sweet To be,
The lady Future of our comrade's love.

    A guest. What rhymes unborn are shut within that
        word!

    Amad. Thus then I soak my heart's dear roots in
        wine,
And the warm drops roll up and down my blood,
Till every tendril of my straying veins
Rings with delight.   [*They drink*
                And now, my sons of Bacchus,
To the delirious dance!—Nay, Torrismond,—
You'll come with us at least.—

    Torris.   To-night, I thank you,
It is against my will; indeed I cannot;
I'm vilely out of tune,—my thoughts are cracked,
And my words dismal. 'Pray you, pardon me:
Some other night we will, like Bacchanals,
Shiver the air with laughter and rough songs,
And be most jovial madmen.

Amad.   Be it so,
If be it must. We bid you, sir, farewell.
    Torris. Good-night, good lads.
        [*Exeunt* AMADEUS *and others: manent* TORRISMOND *and* CYRANO
                                        Now go, dear Cyrano;
Let me not keep you by my wayward mood.—
    Cyrano. If it does not offend you, suffer me—
    Torris. Offend me! No; thou dost not, Cyrano;
I do offend myself. Hadst thou but eyes
To see the spirit toiling in this breast,
How low a wretch should I appear to thee;
How pitifully weak! Now tell me, sir,—
I shrink not from the truth, although it stab,
And beg it from your mouth,—what think you of me?
    Cyrano. Of you, my lord?
    Torris. Yes, yes; my words, my manners,
My disposition, will,—how seem they to you?
    Cyrano. Sir, my heart speaks of you as one most kind;
Spirited and yet mild: a man more noble
Breathes not his maker's air.
    Torris.   Stay, my good friend;
I did not ask for flattery.
    Cyran.   Nor I answer it;
Saying, that here I shake him by the hand
That has no better in humanity:
A fine, free spirit.
    Torris.   You had better say
A whirring, singing, empty wine-bubble,
Like one of these that left us. So I was;
Vain, futile, frivolous; a boy, a butterfly,—
In semblance: but inside, by heaven! a depth

Of thoughts most earnest, an unfuelled flame
Of self-devouring love. Cyrano, Cyrano,
I yearn, and thirst, and ache to be beloved,
As I could love,—through my eternal soul,
Immutably, immortally, intensely,
Immeasurably. Oh! I am not at home
In this December world, with men of ice,
Cold sirs and madams. That I had a heart,
By whose warm throbs of love to set my soul!
I tell thee I have not begun to live,
I'm not myself, till I've another self
To lock my dearest, and most secret thoughts in;
Change petty faults, and whispering pardons with;
Sweetly to rule, and Oh! most sweetly serve.—
   Cyrano. Have you no father,—nor a friend? Yet I,
I, Torrismond, am living, and the duke.
   Torris. Forgive me, sir, forgive me: I am foolish;
I've said I know not what, I know not why;
'Tis nothing,—fancies; I'll to bed;—'tis nothing;
Worth but a smile, and then to be forgotten.
Good-night: to-morrow I will laugh at this.
   Cyrano. I'll say no more but that I hope you will.
                                           [*Exit*
   Torris. I knew it would be so. He thinks me now
Weak, unintelligible, fanciful—
A boy shut up in dreams, a shadow-catcher:
So let him think. My soul is where he sees not,
Around, above, below. Yes, yes; the curse
Of being for a little world too great,
Demanding more than nature has to give,
And drinking up, for ever and in vain,

The shallow, tasteless skimmings of their love,
Through this unfathomable fever here.—
A thought of comfort comes this way; its warmth
I feel, although I see it not. How's this?
There's something I half know; yes, I remember,—
The feast last night: a dear, ingenuous girl
Poured soft, smooth hope upon my dashing passions,
Until they tossed their billowy selves to sleep.
I'll see her, try her: in this very garden
Often she walks; thither I'll bear my wishes,
And may she prove the echo of their craving!   [*Exit*

SCENE III. *A garden by moonlight*

VERONICA, ELVIRA *and other female attendants*

Veron. Come then, a song; a winding, gentle song,
To lead me into sleep. Let it be low
As zephyr, telling secrets to his rose,
For I would hear the murmuring of my thoughts;
And more of voice than of that other music
That grows around the strings of quivering lutes;
But most of thought; for with my mind I listen,
And when the leaves of sound are shed upon it,
If there's no seed, remembrance grows not there.
So life, so death: a song, and then a dream!
Begin before another dewdrop fall
From the soft hold of these disturbed flowers,
For sleep is filling up my senses fast,
And from these words I sink.

SONG

How many times do I love thee, dear?
　　Tell me how many thoughts there be
　　　　In the atmosphere
　　　　Of a new-fall'n year,
　　Whose white and sable hours appear
　　　　The latest flake of Eternity:—
So many times do I love thee, dear.

How many times do I love again?
　　Tell me how many beads there are
　　　　In a silver chain
　　　　Of evening rain,
　　Unravelled from the tumbling main,
　　　　And threading the eye of a yellow star:—
So many times do I love again.

Elvira. She sees no longer: leave her then alone,
Encompassed by this round and moony night.
A rose-leaf for thy lips, and then good-night:
So life, so death: a song, and then a dream!

　　　　　　　[*Exeunt* ELVIRA *and attendants, leaving* VERONICA *asleep*

Enter TORRISMOND

Torris. Herself! her very self, slumbering gently!
Sure sleep is turned to beauty in this maid,
And all the rivalry of life and death
Makes love upon her placid face. And here,
How threads of blue, wound off yon thorny stars
That grow upon the wall of hollow night,
Flow o'er each sister-circle of her bosom,
Knotting themselves into a clue for kisses

Up to her second lip. There liquid dimples
Are ever twinkling, and a sigh has home
Deep in their red division,—a soft sigh,
Scarce would it bow the summer-weeds, when they
Play billows in the fields, and pass a look
Of sunshine through their ranks from sword to sword.
Gracefully bending. On that cheek the blush
That ever dawns dares be no common blush,
But the faint ghost of some dishevelled rose
Unfurls its momentary leaves, and bursts
So quick the haunted fairness knows it not.
O that this gaze could be eternity!
And yet a moment of her love were more.
Were there infection in the mind's disease,
Inoculation of a thought, even now
Should she, from all the windings of her dream,
Drink my impetuous passion, and become
All that I ask. Break from your buds, dear eyes,
And draw me into you.
    Veron. (*awaking*).   Who's there? I dreamt:—
As I do love that broad, smooth-edged star,
And her young, vandyked moons that climb the night
Round their faint mother, I would not have had
Another eye peeping upon that dream,
For one of them to wear upon my breast;
And I'll not whisper it, for fear these flags
Should chance to be the green posterity
Of that eaves-dropping, woman-witted grass,
That robbed the snoring wasps of their least voice,
To teach their feathery gossips of the air
What long, and furry ears king Midas sprouted;

And I'll not think of it, for meditation
Oft presses from the heart its inmost wish,
And thaws its silence into straying words.
    Torris. (*aside*). I am no man, if this dream were not
      spun
By the very silk-worm that doth make his shop
In Cupid's tender wing-pit, and winds fancies
In lovers' corner thoughts, when grandam Prudence
Has swept the hearth of passion, thrown on cinders,
And gone to bed:—and she is not a woman,
If this same secret, buried in her breast,
Haunt not her tongue,—and hark! here comes its
      ghost.
    Veron. A fable and a dream! Here, in this garden,
It seemed I was a lily:—
    Torris. (*aside*).   So you are,
But fitter for Arabian paradise,
Or those arched gardens where pale-petalled stars,
With sunlight honeying their dewy cores,
Tremble on sinuous, Corinthian necks,—
Where Morn her roses feeds, her violets Night.
    Veron. And to my lily-ship a wooer came,
Sailing upon the curvous air of morn,
(For 'twas a sunny dream, and a May sky
The lid of it;) and this imagined suitor,
A glass-winged, tortoise-shell, heart-broken bee,
Was—he you know of, heart. How did he bend
His slender knee, doffing his velvet cap,
And swearing, by the taste of Venus' lip,
If I did not accept his airy love,
The truest heart, that ever told the minutes

Within an insect's breast, should shed its life
Around the hilt of his unsheathed sting.
And then this tiny thunderer of flowers,
Quite, quite subdued, let down a string of tears,
(Little they were, but full of beeish truth,)
Almost a dew-drop-much, on the fair pages
Of transmigrated me; whereon, O Love!
Thou tamed'st the straightest prude of Flora's
    daughters;
For I did pity Torrismond the bee.
And let him, if his life lived in my love,
Have that for courtesy.—
    Torris. (coming forward). O lady! then
Will you deny him now? when here he kneels,
And vows by heaven, and by the sacred souls
Of all the dead and living, in your pity
His hope is folded, in your soul his love,
And in that love his everlasting life.
    Veron. Out on my tongue, the naughty runaway!
What has he heard? Now, if this man should be
Vain, selfish, light, or hearted with a stone,
Or worthless any way, as there are many,
I've given myself, like alms unto an idiot,
To be for nothing squandered.
    Torris.   Lady, speak!
And for my truth, O that my mind were open,
My soul expressed and written in a book,
That thou might'st read and know! Believe, believe me!
And fear me not, for, if I speak not truth,
May I speak never more, but be struck dumb!
May I be stripped of manhood and made devil,

If I mean not as truly unto thee,
Though bold it be, as thou unto thyself!
I will not swear, for thou dost know that easy:
But put me to the proof, say, "kill thyself";
I will outlabour Hercules in will,
And in performance, if that waits on will.
Shall I fight sword-less with a youthful lion?
Shall I do ought that I may die in doing?
Oh! were it possible for such an angel,
I almost wish thou hadst some impious task,
That I might act it and be damned for thee.
But, earned for thee, perdition's not itself,
Since all that has a taste of thee in it
Is blest and heavenly.
    Veron.   Stop! You frighten me:
I dare not doubt you.
    Torris.   Dare not? Can you so?
    Veron. I dare not, for I cannot. I believe you:
It is my duty.
    Torris.   To the dutiful
Their duty is their pleasure. Is it not?
    Veron. 'Twas a rash word; it rather is my fate.
    Torris. It is my fate to love; thou art my fate.
So be not adverse.
    Veron.   How can I say further?
I do believe you: less I'll not avow,
And more I cannot.
    Torris.   Stay, Veronica!
This very night we both of us may die,
Or one at least: and it is very likely
We never meet; or, if we meet, not thus,

But somehow hindered by the time, the place,
The persons. There are many chances else,
That, though no bigger than a sunny mote,
Coming between may our whole future part,—
With Milo's force tear our existence up,
And turn away the branches of each life,
Even from this hour, on whose star-knotted trunk
We would engraft our union! it may sever us
As utterly as if the world should split
Here, as we stand, and all Eternity
Push through the earthquake's lips, and rise between us.
Then let us know each other's constancy:
Thou in my mind, and I in thine shall be;
And so [in]disseparable to the edge
Of thinnest lightning.—
    Veron.   Stay: be answered thus.
If thou art Torrismond, the brain of feather;
If thou art light and empty Torrismond,
The admiration, oath, and patron-saint
Of frivolous revellers, he whose corky heart,
Pierced by a ragged pen of Cupid's wing,
Spins like a vane upon his mother's temple
In every silly sigh,—let it play on:—
    Torris. It is not so; I vow, Veronica—
    Veron. If you unpeopled the Olympian town
Of all its gods, and shut them in one oath,
It would not weigh a flue of melting snow
In my opinion. Listen thus much more:
If thou art otherwise than all have held
Except myself; if these, which men do think
The workings of thy true concentrate self,

Have been indeed but bubbles raised in sport
By the internal god, who keeps unseen
The fountains of thine undiscovered spirit;
If, underneath this troubled scum of follies,
Lies what my hopes have guessed:—why, guess thy
    wishes,
What it may be unto Veronica.
   Torris. What need of doubts and guesses? make me
    firm;
With fixed assurance prop my withering hopes,
Or tear them up at once: give truth for truth.
I know it is the custom to dissemble,
Because men's hearts are shallow, and their nature
So mean, ill-nurtured, selfish, and debased,
They needs must paint and swaddle them in lies,
Before the light could bear to look upon them.
But as thou art, thus unalloyed and fresh,
From thy divine creation, soul and body,
Tread artifice to dust, and boldly speak
Thine innocent resolve.
   Veron.   Thus then I say:
As I believe thee steadfast and sincere,
(And, if it be not so, God pity me!)
I love thee dearly, purely, heartily;
So witness heaven, and our own silent spirits!
   Torris. And by my immortality I swear,
With the like honesty, the like to thee,
Thou picture of the heavens!
   Veron.   Hark! some one comes:—
Now we must part. Henceforth remember thou,
How in this azure secresy of night,

And with what vows, we here have dedicated
Ourselves, and our eternity of being,
Unto each other in our maker's presence.
Good-night, then, Torrismond.
   Torris.   And such to thee,
As thou to me hast given, fairest fair!
Best good! of thy dear kind most ever dear!

                                   [Exeunt severally

      SCENE IV.   *An apartment in the ducal palace*
          Enter the DUKE *and courtiers*

   Duke. Yes, was it not enough, good Garcia,—
Blood spilt in every street by his wild sword;
The reverend citizens pelted with wrongs,
Their rights and toil-worn honours blown aside,
Torn off, and trampled 'neath his drunken foot;
The very daughters of the awful church
Smeared in their whiteness by his rude attempts;
The law thus made a lie even in my mouth;
Myself a jest for beer-pot orators;
My state dishonoured;—was it not enough
To turn a patience, made of ten-years' ice,
Into a thunderbolt?
   Garcia.   It was too much:
I wonder at your Grace's long endurance.
Did you ne'er chide him?
   Duke.   No, never in his life;
He has not that excuse. My eyes and ears
Were frozen-closed. Yet was it not enough
That his ill deeds outgrew all name and number,
O'erflowed his years and all men's memories?

                             10-2

Gaudentio, I was mild; I bore upon me
This world of wrongs, and smiled. But mark you now,
How he was grateful.—Tell them, Melchior.
  Melch. Linked, as it is surmised, with Lutherans,
And other rebels 'gainst his father's state,
He has not only for their aid obtained
From me, the steward of the dukedom, money,
But also robbed, most treacherously robbed,
By night, and like a thief, the public treasury.
  Gauden. I'll not believe it; and he is a villain,
Ay, and the very thief, that did the thing,
Who brings the accusation.
  Duke.   Knave, I think
Thou wert my son's accomplice.
  Melch.   Nay, my lord,
He says what all would say, and most myself,
But that these facts—
  Gauden.   What facts? What witnesses?
Who saw? Who heard? Who knows?
  Duke.   Our trusty steward.
  Gauden. A Spanish Jew! a godless, heartless exile,
Whose ear's the echo of the whispering world.
Why, if *he* only knows, and saw, and heard,
This Argus-witness, with his blood-hound nose,
Who keeps a fairy in his upright ear,
Is no more than a black, blind, ugly devil,
Nick-named a lie.
  Duke.   Be silent, slave, or dead.
I do believe him: Garcia, so dost thou?
All honest men, good Melchior, like thyself,—

For that thou art, I think, upon my life,—
Believe thee too.
  Melch.   It is my humble trust:
And, in the confidence of honesty,
I pray you pardon this good servant's boldness.
(*Aside*). God help the miserable velvet fellow!
It seems he has forgot that little story,
How he debauched my poor, abandoned sister,
And broke my family into the grave.—
That's odd; for I exceeding well remember it,
Though then a boy.
  Duke.   Gaudentio, thou dost hear
Why I forgive thee: but be cautious, sir.
  Gauden. Cautious,—but honest,—cautious of a
    villain.
  Duke. No more!—But see where comes the man
  we talk of.
Leave us together.   [*Exeunt courtiers*

     Enter TORRISMOND

      Torrismond, well met!—
  Torris. Why then well parted, for I'm going to bed.
I'm weary; so, good-night.
  Duke. Stay; I must speak to you.—
  Torris. To-morrow then, good father, and all day.
But now no more than the old sleepy word,
And so again, good-night.
  Duke.   Turn, sir, and stay:
I will be brief, as brief as speech can be.—
Seek elsewhere a good night: there is none here.
This is no home for your good nights, bad son,

Who hast made evil all my days to come,
Poisoned my age, torn off my beauteous hopes
And fed my grave with them.—Oh! thou hast now,
This instant, given my death an hundred sinews,
And drawn him nearer by a thousand hours.
But what of that? You'd sow me like a grain,
And from my stalk pick you a ducal crown.
But I will live.—
    Torris.   That you may live and prosper
Is every day my prayer, my wish, my comfort.
But what offence has raised these cruel words?
    Duke. That I may live, you plot against my life;
That I may prosper, you have cured my fortunes
Of their encrusted jaundice,—you have robbed me.
So, for your prayers and wishes I do thank you;
But for your deeds I wish and pray Heaven's vengeance.
    Torris. Is this your own invention, or—O nature!
O love of fathers! could a father hear
His offspring thus accused, and yet believe?
Believe! Could he endure, and not strike dead,
The monster of the lie? Sir, here or there,
In you, or your informers, there's a villain,
A fiend of falsehood: so beware injustice!
    Duke. I never was unjust, but when I pardoned
Your bloody sins and ravening appetites,—
For which Heaven pardon me, as I repent it!
But I'll not play at battledore with words.
Hear me, young man, in whom I did express
The venom of my nature, thus the son,
Not of my virtuous will, but foul desires,
Not of my life, but of a wicked moment,

Not of my soul, but growing from my body,
Like thorns or poison on a wholesome tree,
The rank excrescence of my tumid sins,—
And so I tear thee off: for, Heaven doth know,
All gentler remedies I have applied;
But to this head thy rankling vice has swelled,
That, if thou dwellest in my bosom longer,
Thou wilt infect my blood, corrode my heart,
And blight my being: therefore, off for ever!

   Torris. O mother, thou art happy in thy grave!
And there's the hell in which my father lies,
The serpent that hath swallowed him!

GAUDENTIO rushes in

   Gauden. (*as he enters, to those without, the other
courtiers, who also enter but remain at the side*).   Away!
Let me come in!...Now, I beseech you, lords,
Put out this anger; lay a night of sleep
Upon its head, and let its pulse of fire
Flap to exhaustion. Do not, sir, believe
This reptile falsehood: think it o'er again,
And try him by yourself; thus questioning,
Could I, or did I, thus, or such a fault,
In my beginning days? There stands before you
The youth and golden top of your existence,
Another life of yours: for, think your morning
Not lost, but given, passed from your hand to his,
The same except in place. Be then to him
As was the former tenant of your age,
When you were in the prologue of your time,
And he lay hid in you unconsciously

Under his life. And thou, my younger master,
Remember there's a kind of god in him,
And after heaven the next of thy religion.
Thy second fears of God, thy first of man,
Are his, who was creation's delegate,
And made this world for thee in making thee.

   Duke. A frost upon thy words, intended dog!
Because thy growth has lost its four-legged way
And wandered with thee into man's resemblance,
Shalt thou assume his rights? Get to thy bed,
Or I'll decant thy pretext of a soul,
And lay thee, worm, where thou shalt multiply.
Sir, slave, your gibbet's sown.

   Torris.   Leave him, Gaudentio,
My father and your master are not here;
His good is all gone hence, he's truly dead;
All that belonged to those two heavenly names
[Is] gone from life with him, and changing cast
This slough behind, which all abandoned sins
Creep into and enliven devilishly.

   Duke. What! stand I in thy shadow? or has Momus
Opened a window 'twixt thy heart and mine?
'Tis plated then!

   Torris.   We talk like fighting boys:—
Out on't! I repent of my mad tongue.
Come, sir; I cannot love you after this,
But we may meet and pass a nodding question—

   Duke. Never! There lies no grain of sand between
My loved and my detested. Wing thee hence,
Or thou dost stand to-morrow on a cob-web
Spun o'er the well of clotted Acheron,

Whose hydrophobic entrails stream with fire;
And may this intervening earth be snow,
And my step burn like the mid coal of Aetna,
Plunging me, through it all, into the core
Where in their graves the dead are shut like seeds,
If I do not—O but he is my son!
If I do not forgive thee then—but hence!
Gaudentio, hence with him, for in my eyes
He does look demons.—

    Melch. (*to Torrismond*). Come out with me and
      leave him:
You will be cool, to-morrow.

    Torris.   That I shall;
Cool as an ice-drop on the skull of Death,
For winter is the season of the tomb,
And that's my country now.

    Duke.   Away with him!
I will not hear.—Where did I leave my book?
Or was it music?—Take the beggar out.
Is there no supper yet?—O my good Melchior!
I'm an eternal gap of misery.—
Let's talk of something else.

    Torris. O father, father! must I have no father,
To think how I shall please, to pray for him,
To spread his virtues out before my thought,
And set my soul in order after them?
To dream, and talk of in my dreaming sleep?
If I have children, and they question me
Of him who was to me as I to them;
Who taught me love, and sports, and childish lore;
Placed smiles where tears had been; who bent his talk,

That it might enter my low apprehension,
And laughed when words were lost.—O father, father!
Must I give up the first word that my tongue,
The only one my heart has ever spoken?
Then take speech, thought, and knowledge quite
    away,—
Tear all my life out of the universe,
Take off my youth, unwrap me of my years,
And hunt me up the dark and broken past
Into my mother's womb: there unbeget me;
For 'till I'm in thy veins and unbegun,
Or to the food returned which made the blood
That did make me, no possible lie can ever
Unroot my feet of thee. Canst thou make nothing?
Then do it here, for I would rather be
At home nowhere, than here nowhere at home.
   Duke. Why ask'st thou me? Hast thou no deeds
    to undo,
No virtues to rebuy, no sins to loose?
Catch from the wind those sighs that thou hast caused;
Out of large ocean pick the very tears,
And set them in their cabinets again.
Renew thyself, and then will I remember
How thou camest thus. Thou art all vices now
Of thine own getting. My son Torrismond
Did sow himself under a heap of crime,
And thou art grown from him: die to the root,
So I may know thee as his grave at least.—
Now, Melchior, we'll away.
   Melch.   Not yet, my lord:
I wait upon this gentleman.

Duke.   Is't so?
Why then, begone! Good-morrow to you, sirs.
Farewell! and be that word a road to death
Uncrossed by any other! Not a word!

Exit with courtiers: manent TORRISMOND *and* MELCHIOR

Melch. Will you not stay?
                              He's gone: but follow not:—
There's not a speck of flesh upon his heart!
What shall we do?
Torris.   What shall we do?—why, all.
How many things, sir, do men live to do?
The mighty labour is to die: we'll do't,—
But we'll drive in a chariot to our graves,
Wheel'd with big thunder, o'er the heads of men.

[*Exeunt*

Act II

Enter TORRISMOND

Torris. Then here's an end of life.

[*End of MS.*]

FRAGMENTS OF
DEATH'S JEST-BOOK[1]

A BEAUTIFUL NIGHT

How lovely is the heaven of this night,
How deadly still its earth! The forest brute
Has crept into his cave, and laid himself
Where sleep has made him harmless like the lamb.
The horrid snake, his venom now forgot,
Is still and innocent as the honied flower
Under his head: and man, in whom are met
Leopard and snake, and all the gentleness
And beauty of the young lamb and the bud,
Has let his ghost out, put his thoughts aside
And lent his senses unto death himself.

SAD AND CHEERFUL SONGS CONTRASTED

Sing me no more such ditties: they are well
For the last gossips, when the snowy wind
Howls in the chimney till the very taper
Trembles with its blue flame, and the bolted gates
Rattle before old winter's palsied hand.
If you will sing, let it be cheerily
Of dallying love. There's many a one among you
Hath sung, beneath our oak trees to his maiden,
Light bird-like mockeries, fit for love in springtime.
Sing such a one.

[1] These were fragments in Beddoes' MSS.

MAN'S ANXIOUS, BUT INEFFECTUAL
GUARD AGAINST DEATH

Luckless man
Avoids the miserable bodkin's point,
And, flinching from the insect's little sting,
In pitiful security keeps watch,
While 'twixt him and that hypocrite the sun,
To which he prays, comes windless pestilence,
Transparent as a glass of poisoned water
Through which the drinker sees his murderer smiling;
She stirs no dust, and makes no grass to nod,
Yet every footstep is a thousand graves,
And every breath of her's as full of ghosts
As a sunbeam with motes.

MOURNERS CONSOLED

Dead, is he? What's that further than a word,
Hollow as is the armour of a ghost
Whose chinks the moon he haunts doth penetrate?
Belief in death is the fell superstition,
That hath appalled mankind and chained it down,
A slave unto the dismal mystery
Which old opinion dreams beneath the tombstone.
Dead is he, and the grave shall wrap him up?
And this you see is he? And all is ended?
Ay *this* is cold, that was a glance of him
Out of the depth of his immortal self;
This utterance and token of his being
His spirit hath let fall, and now is gone
To fill up nature and complete her being.

A GREAT SACRIFICE SELF-COMPENSATED

True I have had much comfort gazing on thee,
Much too perhaps in thinking I might have thee
Nearly myself, a fellow soul to live with.
But, weighing well man's frail and perilous tenure
Of all good in the restless, wavy world,
Ne'er dared I set my soul on any thing
Which but a touch of time can shake to pieces.
Alone in the eternal is my hope.
Took I thee? that intensest joy of love
Would soon grow fainter and at last dissolve.
But, if I yield thee, there is something done
Which from the crumbling earth my soul divorces,
And gives it room to be a greater spirit.
There is a greater pang, methinks, in nature
When she takes back the life of a dead world,
Than when a new one severs from her depth
Its bright, revolving birth. So I'll not hoard thee,
But let thee part, reluctant, though in hope
That greater happiness will thence arise.

FRAGMENTS OF THE LAST MAN

DIANEME *and female attendants*

* * *

Attend. The tide of darkness now is at its height.
Yon lily-woven cradle of the hours
Hath floated half her shining voyage, nor yet
Is by the current of the morn opposed.

* * *

Dianeme. Now, maids, farewell; this is the very
    echo
Of his expiring time; one snowy cloud
Hangs, like an avalanche of frozen light,
Upon the peak of night's cerulean Alp,
And yon still pine, a bleak anatomy,
Flows, like a river, on the planet's disk,
With its black, wandering arms. Farewell to all;
There is my hand to weep on.
                              Now my soul
Develops its great beams, and, like a cloud
Racked by the mighty winds, at once expands
Into a measureless, immortal growth.
Crescented night, and amethystine stars,
And day, thou god and glory of the heavens,
Flow on for ever! Play, ye living spheres,
Through the infinity of azure wafted
On billowy music! Airs immortal, strew
Your tressèd beauty on the clouds and seas!

And thou the sum of these, nature of all,
Thou providence pervading the whole space
Of measureless creation; thou vast mind,
Whose thoughts these pageantries and seasons are,
Who claspest all in one imagination,
All hail! I too am an eternity;
I am an universe. My soul is bent
Into a girdling circle full of days;
And my fears rise through the deep sky of it,
Blossoming into palpitating stars;
And suns are launched, and planets wake within me;
The words upon my breath are showery clouds,
Sailing along a summer; Casimir
Is the clear truth of ocean, to look back
The beams of my soft love, the world to turn
Within my blue embrace. I am an heaven,
And he my breezes, rays, and harmony;
'Round and around the curvous atmosphere
Of my own real existence I revolve,
Serene and starry with undying love.
I am, I have been, I shall be, O glory!
An universe, a god, a living Ever.   [*She dies*

RECEPTION OF EVIL TIDINGS

What's this? Did you not see a white convulsion
Run through his cheek and fling his eye-lids up?
There's mischief in the paper.
                              Mark again
How, with that open palm, he shades his brain
From its broad, sudden meaning. Once I saw

One who had dug for treasure in a corner,
Where he, by torchlight, saw a trembling man
Burying a chest at night. Just so he stood
With open striving lips and shaking hair;
Alive but in his eyes, and they were fixed
On a smeared, earthy, bleeding corpse—his sister,
There by her murderer crushed into the earth.

A RUFFIAN

There's a fellow
With twisting root-like hair up to his eyes,
And they are streaked with red and starting out
Under their bristling brows; his crooked tusks
Part, like a hungry wolf's, his cursing mouth;
His head is frontless, and a swinish mane
Grows o'er his shoulders:—brown and warty hands,
Like roots, with pointed nails.—He is the man.

A CROCODILE

Hard by the lilied Nile I saw
A duskish river-dragon stretched along,
The brown habergeon of his limbs enamelled
With sanguine almandines and rainy pearl:
And on his back there lay a young one sleeping,
No bigger than a mouse; with eyes like beads,
And a small fragment of its speckled egg
Remaining on its harmless, pulpy snout;
A thing to laugh at, as it gaped to catch
The baulking, merry flies. In the iron jaws
Of the great devil-beast, like a pale soul

Fluttering in rocky hell, lightsomely flew
A snowy troculus, with roseate beak
Tearing the hairy leeches from his throat.

"BONA DE MORTUIS"

Ay, ay; *good man, kind father, best of friends*—
These are the words that grow, like grass and nettles,
Out of dead men, and speckled hatreds hide,
Like toads, among them.

SPEAKER'S MEANING DIMLY DESCRIED

I know not whether
I see your meaning: if I do, it lies
Upon the wordy wavelets of your voice,
Dim as an evening shadow in a brook,
When the least moon has silver on't no larger
Than the pure white of Hebe's pinkish nail.

ANTICIPATION OF EVIL TIDINGS

I fear there is some maddening secret
Hid in your words, (and at each turn of thought
Comes up a skull,) like an anatomy
Found in a weedy hole, 'mongst stones and roots
And straggling reptiles, with his tongueless mouth
Telling of murder.

A DREAM

Last night I looked into a dream; 'twas drawn
On the black midnight of a velvet sleep,
And set in woeful thoughts; and there I saw
A thin, pale Cupid, with bare, ragged wings
Like skeletons of leaves, in autumn left,
That sift the frosty air. One hand was shut,
And in its little hold of ivory
Fastened a May-morn zephyr, frozen straight,
Made deadly with a hornet's rugged sting,
Gilt with the influence of an adverse star.
Such was his weapon, and he traced with it,
Upon the waters of my thoughts, these words:
"I am the death of flowers, and nightingales,
And small-lipped babes, that give their souls to summer
To make a perfumed day with: I shall come,
A death no larger than a sigh to thee,
Upon a sunset hour."—And so he passed
Into the place where faded rainbows are,
Dying along the distance of my mind;
As down the sea Europa's hair-pearls fell
When through the Cretan waves, the curly bull
Dashed, tugging at a stormy plough, whose share
Was of the northern hurricane——

EXTREME ACCLIVITY

Its impossible ascent was steep,
As are the million pillars of a shower,
Torn, shivered, and dashed hard against the earth,
When Day no longer breathes, but through the hours
The ghost of chaos haunts the ruined sky.

RAIN

The blue, between yon star-nailed cloud
The double-mountain and this narrow valley,
Is strung with rain, like a fantastic lyre.

LIFE'S UNCERTAINTY

* * *

A. The crevice 'twixt two after-dinner minutes,
The crack between a pair of syllables,
May sometimes be a grave as deep as 'tis
From noon to midnight in the hoop of time.
But for this man, his life wears ever steel
From which disease drops blunted. If indeed
Death lay in the market-place, or were—but hush!
See you the tremble of that myrtle bough?
Does no one listen?
B.   Nothing with a tongue:
The grass is dumb since Midas, and no Aesop
Translates the crow or hog. Within the myrtle
Sits a hen-robin, trembling like a star,
Over her brittle eggs.
A.   Is it no more?
B. Nought: let her hatch.

KISSES

Her kisses are
Soft as a snow-tuft in the dewless cup
Of a redoubled rose, noiselessly falling
When heaven is brimful of starry night.

FRAGMENTS OF
LOVE'S ARROW POISONED

SCENE I

ERMINIA and female attendant

Attend. Come lift your head from that sad pillow,
    lady,
Let comfort kiss thee dry. Nay, weep no more:
Oh! sure thy brain has emptied all its tears,
Thy breast outsighed its passion, leaving room
For sleep to pour her sweetness into them,
And the cored sleep of sleep, tranquillity,
That opens but one window of the soul,
And, with her hand on sorrow's face, does keep her
Dark in her bed and dayless. Quiet now—
Will you take peace?
    Ermin.   Good-night; you must go in:
The door of life is shut upon me now;
I'm sepulchred alone. Look in the west;
Mark you the dusty, weary traveller,
That stumbles down the clouds?
    Attend.   I see the sun
Silently dying.
    Ermin.   Weep till your sight is found.—
I have been one that thought there was a sun,
A joyful heat-maker; and, like a child
By a brook's side spooning the sparkles out,
I caught at his reflection in my soul,
And found 'twas water painted with a lie,

Cold, bitter water; I have cried it out.
Sometimes you may see some one through the clouds
Stepping about the sky,—and then, in sooth,
He robs some mountain of its child, the day,
And lays it at the sea's door: but for that
I' the west, 'tis the fat, unwholesome star,
The bald fool-planet, that has men upon it,
And they nickname it "world".
And oh! this humpy bastard of the sun,
It was my slave, my dog, and in my lap
Laid down its load of pleasure every night,
And spun me sunshine to delight my eyes,—
Carried my cities, and did make me summer,
And flower-limbed spring, and groves with shady
      autumn:
But now the whelp rolls up his woody back,
And turns it on me, and so trundles down,
Leaving this bit of rock for me to live on,
And his round shadow to be cold in. Go!
Follow the rabble clinging at his heels,
Get thee a seat among his rags.—Dost know
That Momus picked a burnt-out comet up
From Vulcan's floor, and stuck a man upon it;
Then, having laught, he flung the wick away,
And let the insect feed on planet oil:—
What was't? Man and his ball.
   Attend.   O dearest lady!
Let not your thoughts find instruments of mirth
So on the shore where reason has been wrecked,
To lay them in your brain along with grief;
For grief and laughter, mingled in the skull,

Oft boil to madness. Did you hear my words?
 Ermin. Ay, comfort was among them,—that's a
  plaything
For girls, a rattle full of noisy lies
To fright away black thoughts, and let the sun
In on the breast. For madness, though I hold it
Kinder to man's enjoyment than true sense,
And I would choose it, if they lay before me,
Even as a grape beside an adder's tongue,
To squeeze into my thoughts as in a cup,
Hating the forked and the bitter truth,—
I cannot find it.
    *   *   *

 Attend.   Indeed your love was much;
Your life but an inhabitant of his.
 Ermin. Loved him! 'tis not enough; the angels
  might,—
They might think what I mean, but could not speak it.
I dreamt it was the day of judgment once,
And that my soul, in fear of hidden sins,
Went with his stolen body on its shoulders,
And stood for him before the judgment-seat:—
O that I now were damned as I was then!
    *   *   *

SCENE IV. *The abyss of Space*

AMBROSIUS *and* CYNTHIA *in the car, returning to the earth.*
AMBROSIUS *loquitur*

O what a deep delight it is to cleave,
Out-darting thought, above all sight and sound,
And sweep the ceiling of the universe,
Thus with our locks! How it does mad the heart,
How dances it along the living veins,
Like hot and steaming wine! How my eyes ache
With gazing on this mighty vacancy!
O Universe of earth and air and ocean,
Which man calls infinite, where art thou now?
Sooner a babe should pierce the marble ear
Of death, and startle his tombed ancestor,
'Mid Hell's thick laughter, shrieks, and flamy noises,
With cradle-pulings, than the gathered voice
Of every thunder, ocean, and wild blast,
Find thee, thou atom, in this wilderness!
This boundless emptiness, this waveless sea,
This desert of vacuity, alone
Is great: and thou, for whom the world was made,
Art as the wren's small goblet of a home
Unto the holy vastness of the temple!

*   *   *

Why, Rome was naked once, a bastard smudge,
Tumbled on straw, the denfellow of whelps,
Fattened on roots, and, when a-thirst for milk,
He crept beneath and drank the swagging udder
Of Tiber's brave she-wolf; and Heaven's Judea
Was folded in a pannier.

DREAM-PEDLARY

I

If there were dreams to sell,
    What would you buy?
Some cost a passing bell;
    Some a light sigh,
That shakes from Life's fresh crown
Only a rose-leaf down.
If there were dreams to sell,
Merry and sad to tell,
And the crier rung the bell,
    What would you buy?

II

A cottage lone and still,
    With bowers nigh,
Shadowy, my woes to still,
    Until I die.
Such pearl from Life's fresh crown
Fain would I shake me down.
Were dreams to have at will,
This would best heal my ill,
    This would I buy.

III

But there were dreams to sell
    Ill didst thou buy;
Life is a dream, they tell,
    Waking, to die.

Dreaming a dream to prize,
Is wishing ghosts to rise;
And, if I had the spell
To call the buried well,
    Which one would I?

IV

If there are ghosts to raise,
    What shall I call,
Out of hell's murky haze,
    Heaven's blue pall?
Raise my loved long-lost boy
To lead me to his joy.—
There are no ghosts to raise;
Out of death lead no ways;
    Vain is the call.

V

Know'st thou not ghosts to sue,
    No love thou hast.
Else lie, as I will do,
    And breathe thy last.
So out of Life's fresh crown
Fall like a rose-leaf down.
Thus are the ghosts to woo;
Thus are all dreams made true,
    Ever to last.

LORD ALCOHOL

I

Who tames the lion now?
Who smoothes Jove's wrinkles now?[1]
Who is the reckless wight
   That in the horrid middle
Of the deserted night
Doth play upon man's brain,
   As on a wanton fiddle,
The mad and magic strain,
The reeling, tripping sound,
To which the world goes round?
   Sing heigh! ho! diddle!
         And then say—
Love, quotha, Love? nay, nay!
It is a spirit fine
Of ale or ancient wine,
   Lord Alcohol, the drunken fay,
        Lord Alcohol alway!

II

Who maketh the pipe-clay man
Think all that nature can?
Who dares the gods to flout,
   Lay fate beneath the table,
And maketh him stammer out
A thousand monstrous things,
   For history a fable,
Dish-clouts for kings?

[1] A rhyme needed: ? "wrinkled brow."

And sends the world along
Singing a ribald song
   Of heigho! Babel?
             Who, I pray—
Love, quotha, Love? nay, nay!
It is a spirit fine
Of ale or ancient wine,
   Lord Alcohol, the drunken fay,
             Lord Alcohol alway!

For EU product safety concerns, contact us at Calle de José Abascal, 56–1°,
28003 Madrid, Spain or eugpsr@cambridge.org.

www.ingramcontent.com/pod-product-compliance
Ingram Content Group UK Ltd.
Pitfield, Milton Keynes, MK11 3LW, UK
UKHW012331130625
459647UK00009B/212